Ethnographic Film

Ethnographic Film

by Karl G. Heider

University of Texas Press Austin & London

Library of Congress Cataloging in Publication Data

Heider, Karl G   1935–
   Ethnographic film.

   Bibliography: p.
   Includes index.
   1. Moving-pictures in ethnology. I. Title.
GN347.H44   301.2'02'08   76–10454
ISBN 0-292-72020-3 (cloth); 0-292-72025-4 (paper)

Second Cloth Printing, 1978
First Paperback Printing, 1978
Second Paperback Printing, 1980

To Gregory Bateson & Margaret Mead

Contents

Preface   ix

Acknowledgments   xiii

1. Introduction   3
Toward a Definition: The Nature of the Category "Ethnographic Film"   3
The Nature of Ethnography   5
The Differing Natures of Ethnography and Film   9
"Truth" in Film and Ethnography   11

2. A History of Ethnographic Film   16
Background Factors   16
Pre-1922   19
Robert Flaherty   20
Grass   25
Scripted Fictional Films   26
Bateson and Mead in Bali and New Guinea   27
Marshall, Gardner, Asch, and Others: Developments at Harvard   30
The French Movement   39
University of California American Indian Series   40
The Netsilik Eskimo Project   41
Australia   42
The Natives' View   42
Institutionalization in the United States   44

3. The Attributes of Ethnographic Film   46
The Attributes   47
The Attributes as Dimensions   97
The Attribute Dimension Grid   112

4. Making Ethnographic Film   118
The Ethics of Ethnographic Filmmaking   118
The Finances of Ethnographic Filmmaking   121
An Ethnographic Film Must Be Based on Ethnographic Understanding   123
Ethnographic Film Must Exploit the Visual Potential of Film   125
Whole Bodies and Whole People in Whole Acts   125

Division of Labor   125
The Meaning of Real Collaboration   126
An Ethnographic Film Cannot Stand by Itself   127
Film versus Videotape   127
Ethnographic Films from Research Footage   128
Preservation of the Film Record   128

5. The Use of Ethnographic Films in Teaching   130
Films and Background Reading   130
Technology   133
Strategies   133

Appendix: A Brief Descriptive Catalogue of Films   135

Bibliography   153

Index   159

Preface

What is "ethnographic film"? The term itself seems to embody an inherent tension or conflict between two ways of seeing and understanding, two strategies for bringing order to (or imposing order on) experience: the scientific and the aesthetic. The evolution of ethnographic filmmaking has been a continuous and ongoing process attempting to reconcile this tension, to achieve a fertile synthesis. Ideally, ethnographic films unite the art and skills of the filmmaker with the trained intellect and insights of the ethnographer. This book examines the implications and the opportunities of such a collaboration; its argument rests on the fundamental assumption that film can be an important medium for the expression of the ethnographic enterprise. What is involved, though, is more demanding than a mere mechanical joining of cinematography and ethnography. There must be interpenetration of disciplines: the cinematographer must accept the scientific demands of ethnography; the ethnographer must adapt his expression to the expanded visual potential of film. Filmmakers must think ethnographically, or scientifically; ethnographers must think cinematographically, or visually. There are great challenges on both sides, and the burgeoning vitality of ethnographic film testifies to the rewards as these challenges are met.

This book is written for people in film, for people in anthropology, and for the increasing number of people who are concerned with both, such as teachers who use these films in their schoolrooms. Most of it is an attempt to develop a systematic way of thinking about ethnographic film, and in particular about the "ethnographicness" of film. The issues which it treats are very close to the concerns of primatologists, sociologists, and psychologists. These neighboring specialists will have little trouble translating it into their own idiom to deal with their own interests.

We have to be very careful when talking of the differences between film and ethnography. We will find enough real problems without fostering an unnecessary rivalry. Three important points should be brought up immediately. First, the simple opposition of scientific ethnography versus artistic cinematography is misleading. Film has its share of science, both in the technology of filmmaking itself and, on another level, in the theorizing about film which has been going on for decades. On the other side, ethnography is a most impure science whose research is carried out by a private field experience. As we think about the natures of film and ethnography in the next chapters, each will shed new and interesting light on the other.

The second major point is that when the demands of ethnography and film seem to conflict and we choose to fulfill the ethnographic demands in order to have a more ethnographic film, the result will probably turn out to be a better film even by cinematographic standards. The ethnographic approach will seem strange at first in some respects to many filmmakers. But I hope to demonstrate that, in the long run, better ethnography will make for better cinematography. And third, although we are thinking about ethnographic film, and developing ways to judge ethnographicness in film, this does not imply any moral superiority for one sort of film over another. There are many worthy sorts of films. This book is about one sort, namely, ethnographic film. Likewise, there are many valid ways to look at human behavior. This book is about one way, namely, ethnography. In short, I am not trying to make over the world film industry along the lines of ethnographic precepts; but at the same time I resist the careless expropriation of the term *ethnographic* to cover any film about people.

A word of explanation about terminology: I use *ethnography* and *anthropology* more or less interchangeably here. Ethnographers are anthropologists who study human behavior. They call themselves ethnographers, ethnologists, social anthropologists, cultural anthropologists, anthropologists, social scientists, or scientists, depending on the context and the audience. Some of them care very deeply about these labels and spend a lot of energy on label clarification. I don't, but I apologize for any offense caused.

There are two rather different uses of film in anthropology. One is the subject of this book, that is, finished films which have been made for public showing and which present some sort of ethnographic understanding. But anthropologists also use the movie camera and the videotape recorder to make visual records of human behavior which can be subjected to detailed, micro- or slow-motion analysis. These raw data are footage or film, but they are not films. After the analysis has been made, the footage may be edited into a film for public presentation of the results of the analysis, as raw material is often incorporated into scientific papers and monographs. Ray L. Birdwhistell's film, *Microcultural Incidents in Ten Zoos*, is one of the few examples of footage which has served both functions. The use of film (and videotape) to make visual records for behavioral analysis has proven to be a powerful innovation, especially in research done by psychologists (for example, see Scheflen 1973). It promises to be an equally powerful tool in anthropological research. But the area of nonverbal behavior research (to use one of its many labels) is a large and complex subject, and, although I shall mention some relevant findings from that general field, I make no attempt to cover the use of footage for analysis.

This book has three characteristics which are not universally admired: it is polemic, it is repetitive, and it speaks in different tongues to different audiences. It might help matters to explain why I feel that each is a useful strategy. It is too soon to write The Definitive Book on ethnographic film. The whole subject is very much in a state of flux, and we need strong statements which organize some of the chaos and offer a next step in thinking about ethnographic film. That is what I have tried to do here. I do not see this book as definitive. My hope is that it will offer some guidance in thinking about ethnographic film.

The repetition comes from a strategy of crisscrossing exposition. The subject of ethnographic film has so many facets that it must be approached from many different directions in order to be at all exhaustive. The problem simply does not lend itself to a logical chain exposition. Thus, the same principle may be treated in one way in the theoretical chapter one, another way in the historical chapter two, yet another way in chapter three, which is on attributes, and then restated in reference to ethnographic filmmakers (chapter four) and to teachers (chapter five). The readers' indulgence for such repetition is begged on the grounds that each reappearance will add to the development of the ideas.

And finally, I am hoping that the various audiences of anthropologists, filmmakers, schoolteachers, and interested others can all be comfortable between the covers of a single book. No one group will want to read every page. But each audience has some concerns in common with each other audience, and in any case it is often good to know what is being said to others.

This is a fairly personal book in the sense that I draw heavily on my own experience in studying the Grand Valley Dani of Irian Jaya, Indonesia (the province has also been called Netherlands New Guinea, West New Guinea, and Irian Barat). I have spent nearly three years doing research among the Dani on four different trips between 1961 and 1970. I have described the Dani in an ethnographic monograph (*The Dugum Dani*) and numerous papers, as well as through two short films (*Dani Sweet Potatoes* and *Dani Houses*), and, during my first months with the Dani, I collaborated with Robert Gardner as he made the film *Dead Birds*. I could never understand my own professors who had done original research but who, from some misguided sense of modesty perhaps, taught only from other people's data and refused to discuss their fieldwork. My own experience as an ethnographer as well as an ethnographic filmmaker is so directly pertinent to a book on ethnographic film that I can hardly pretend noninvolvement. Also, I know my own ethnography and my own films better than I do anyone else's. And I can criticize them with impunity.

Should a book on ethnographic film include photographs or not? I finally decided against it. It could have photographs of the various filmmakers, cameras at hand, standing on location: interesting, but not essential. It could have "production stills" of the sort displayed outside movie theaters. These are still shots which were taken during the filming, but which rarely show scenes that are actually in the film itself. Or it could have photographs printed directly from frames in the film, but necessarily of poor technical quality by the time they reached the printed page. However, the real problem with still photographs in a book like this is that we are concerned with the problems which emerge from trying to make sense out of long sequences of moving pictures, while a still photograph is, after all, still. Ideally there would be a short film to illustrate the principles discussed here.

Inevitably a work such as this one puts great demands on the readers' imagination because of the constant reference to scenes from various ethnographic films. I have tried to keep the references limited to those films which are best known and most widely available. (The film catalogue in the Appendix will be of help here.) And I have tried to make the references explicit enough so that even readers who cannot view the films will be able to visualize the scenes.

Acknowledgments

During the last fifteen years I have shamelessly lifted ideas about ethnographic film from countless sources. I can only begin to do justice in acknowledging those who have contributed in one way or another to this book.

First and foremost, I am indebted to Robert Gardner, who introduced me to ethnographic film and invited me to accompany him to New Guinea. Like so many others, I have benefited tremendously from his time, energy, and insights, all most generously given.

Teaching a course jointly with someone else can be a strenuous educational experience for all concerned, and I have learned much from interactions with my many coteachers in ethnographic film courses: Robert Gardner (Harvard, 1966); Henry Breitrose (Stanford, 1972); Jay Ruby, Sol Worth, and Carroll Williams (Summer Institute for Visual Anthropology, 1972); Richard Hawkins and John Bohm (University of California, Los Angeles, 1973–1974); and John Heider (University of California, Berkeley, Extension, 1974). Others whose influence has been especially important are Timothy Asch, Donald Rundstrom, Ronald Rundstrom, Alan Lomax, and the participants in the Summer Institute for Visual Anthropology in Santa Fe, 1972.

For their comments on earlier versions of this book I am particularly grateful to Ernest Callenbach, Bambi Schieffelin, Robert Gardner, Paul Ekman, Henry Breitrose, and Cameron Macauley.

The final version of this book was finished during the fall of 1975, when I was a Fellow at the Center for Advanced Study in the Behavioral Sciences in Stanford, California. My warm thanks go to that most humane of institutions.

Ethnographic film as a field is unique. I know of no other field where people care so deeply and differ so bitterly. It does make things exciting. But not only do I take the usual responsibility for the content of this book, I should emphasize that among those mentioned above some have opposed this approach most vigorously and in their opposition have helped me to bring things into focus.

I would venture to say that everyone in ethnographic film—indeed in visual anthropology as a whole—can agree on one thing: that we share our indebtedness to Gregory Bateson and Margaret Mead. Jointly and separately they have pioneered in these fields, as in so many other realms of the social sciences, and today, forty years after they went to Bali, they are still at the frontier of our discipline. To them goes an overwhelming acknowledgment.

Ethnographic Film

Chapter 1

Introduction

Toward a Definition: The Nature of the Category "Ethnographic Film"

What do we mean by "ethnographic film"? It is always comfortable to have a concise definition of title phrases. However, this desire for precision can often be dangerous. Of all the words which have been spilled over the definition of ethnographic film, most have treated *ethnographic* as an absolute, present-or-absent characteristic. Let us instead think of ethnographic as a continuously variable property of many films. Throughout this book I use the term *ethnographicness* to talk about films. The term is not particularly euphonious, but it does serve notice that *ethnographic* has a very specific meaning.

The analogy to "tall buildings" is apt here. Tallness is obviously an attribute of buildings. It makes a great deal of difference to an architect, a builder, or an occupant just how tall a building is. They all need to have ways to measure and discuss tallness. But it would make no sense at all to attempt to define tall buildings so that some buildings were "tall" and some "not tall." In the past we have spent much energy trying to define ethnographic film in this way. Now we need to rethink the basic problem of defining ethnographic film.

As long as we phrased the questions in the form "What is an ethnographic film?" or "Is X an ethnographic film?" we were assuming the existence of a bounded category. We had to direct our energies to discovering the boundaries, and we had as our goal the definition of a set of boundary criteria which would allow us to mark off some films as "ethnographic" and, at least implicitly, the rest as "not ethnographic." Certainly the underlying problems are real, but the terms of the inquiry have been sterile. I would suggest a moratorium on such questions.

We can talk about the degree of ethnographicness of a film. So a useful approach is to look for the attributes, or dimensions, of ethnographicness in films.

Adopting this strategy, we should ask "What features make films more or less ethnographic?" and "How ethnographic is this film?" The idea, then, is not to define an ethnographic box-category, but to make explicit those features which contribute to the ethnographicness of films.

There are two overriding considerations:

1. How closely can films approach the highest standards and goals of ethnography? And

2. How can films present information which written ethnographies cannot?

To resolve the apparent paradox of these two considerations, we can rephrase them as follows:

How can the (visual capability of) film complement the (lexical capability of) ethnography?

The truism that "a single picture is worth ten thousand words" can be inverted as "a single word can be worth ten thousand pictures." Depending on the situation, either may be true. The challenge of ethnographic film is to develop ways of thinking about film which will make it more ethnographic.

Even though we refuse to define ethnographic film, we must make explicit those criteria by which we can term some films more ethnographic than others. This will make possible a criticism of films from an ethnographic standpoint. More important for the future, it will allow us to explain clearly to ethnographers and to filmmakers how to make films which are more ethnographic, and thereby more valuable to anthropology.

In evaluating the degree of ethnographicness in any film, or in designing film projects which are maximally ethnographic, we need to consider a number of attributes, some of which emerge from primarily ethnographic constraints, and some of which emerge from cinematographic constraints. We must stress early and often that when we are talking about "ethnographic film," ethnography must take precedence over cinematography. If ethnographic demands conflict with cinematographic demands, ethnography must prevail.

There are lots of ways to skirt around this issue, but it really must be faced head-on. In ethnographic film, film is the tool and ethnography the goal. I have talked with filmmakers who see film as somehow an end in itself, and they reject this idea as demeaning to the art of cinematography. I think that they misunderstand film. It is always a tool for *something*, and in talking about ethnographic film we are just making that something more explicit than usual. But certainly there is an opposite danger: that anthropologists will see film as "only a tool" and not give it the respect and attention which a fine tool demands. Film-the-tool does some things magnificently well, but for other things it is quite inadequate. We have to understand enough so that we do not try to saw wood with a hammer.

Sometimes this matter is phrased as an inevitable contradiction between art and science, with filmmakers arguing the case for art, and anthropologists the case for science. But this is a false and distracting approach. The analogy with ethnography-as-literature is pertinent here. We do not demand that an ethnography be written in great literary style. However, when poor writing obscures the ethnographic point we rightly object. Similarly, although we need not hold ethnographic films to the highest cinematographic standards, a minimal cinematographic competence is required in order that the film communicate at all. In fact, however, if one surveys the 460 films included in the catalogue *Films for Anthropological Teaching* (K. G. Heider 1972c) and those not included, it seems clear that films which are cinematographically incompetent are also ethnographically incompetent (even when made by an ethnographer). Most of the films which we use are far more successful in a technical cinematographic sense than they are in any ethnographic terms. The main problem, and the one to which this book is devoted, is to show filmmakers as well as ethnographers what it means to say that films are ethnographic.

Ethnographic film must be judged in relation to ethnography, which is, after all, a scientific enterprise. In some sense we could say that all films are "ethnographic": they are about people. Even films which only show clouds or lizards have been made by people and therefore say something about the culture of the individuals who made them and who use them. There are many films which have little pretension to ethnographicness but which are of great interest to the ethnographer. I personally feel that *The Last Picture Show*, about the high school class of 1952 in a small Texas town, is a statement which captures the culture of my own high school class of 1952 in Lawrence, Kansas. Likewise, *The Harder They Come* (about Jamaica), *Scenes from a Marriage* (about middle-class Swedish marriage), or *Tokyo Story* all present important truths about cultural situations. As statements (native statements, in fact) about culture, these films are important, and they could very easily be used as raw data or documents in ethnographic research. I am tempted to call them more than just "raw data" and think of them as "naïve ethnography." They have ethnographic import without attempting the science of ethnography. They are good entertainment, but also they are certainly worthy of serious consideration. I have sometimes used such films in my anthropology classes. However, I shall not pay much attention to them here, since I want to consider films which are more specifically and intentionally ethnographic.

The Nature of Ethnography

The most important attribute of ethnographic film is the degree to which it is informed by ethnographic understanding. It would be difficult to define ethnography in a few words, but we must discuss those features of ethnography which are most relevant to ethnographic filmmaking.

First, ethnography is a way of making a detailed description and analysis of human behavior based on a long-term observational study on the spot. A "come-in-shooting-and-get-out-fast" approach and an intuitive-aesthetic appreciation of behavior and people are other sorts of approaches, and, while they may well result in beautiful films, these must inevitably be ethnographically shallow. *The Nuer* is a good example of the dangers of the last approach. It was shot in the late 1960s among a group of Nilotic cattle herders who were living in Ethiopia. Although the filmmakers spent several months on location and captured the pace of life in a cattle camp, their ignorance of Nuer ethnography is obvious throughout the film. There is a sequence of the boys' initiation which is dramatic and moving, but from any ethnographic standpoint it is incomplete. On the most obvious level, the two boys are shown leaving boyhood, but their entrance to manhood is omitted except for a slight reference in the narration. What in the world did the filmmakers think a boys' initiation was all about? The specific important steps in Nuer initiation ceremonies and the structural relation of these ceremonies to rites of passage in general, both of which are well known in ethnographic literature, are hardly touched on in the film. The initiation sequence could have been shaped by these understandings without sacrificing any of the aesthetic qualities of the film. The result would have been much more ethnographically valid.

Another essential feature of ethnography is that it relates specific observed behavior to cultural norms. Many documentary films devote much time to the portrayal of an individual person or event but fall short of the cultural step, putting those data into a cultural context. General cultural statements are especially challenging since they must almost inevitably be made in words, while film is by nature specific and visual. The difficulty of saying no or asking a question through purely visual means in film or photograph has often been remarked. A photographic generalization is almost as hard to achieve. One of the rare attempts occurs in *The Nuer*, where several quick sequences illustrate various tobacco pipes, ornaments, and scar patterns. The most common solution, used in most films, is to have the narrator read words which put the specific visual images into generalized cultural context. But this forces the film to take on some of the quality of a book, at the expense of the purity of its imagery. There is a real temptation to load too much information into the narration, further weakening the "filmicness" of the film, and at times even contradicting the visual information.

A third basic principle of ethnography is holism. To some degree things and events must be understood in their social and cultural context. From this principle come the related dicta of "whole bodies," "whole people," and "whole acts." They emphasize the ethnographic need to present bodies, personalities, and behavior in context. Isolated closeups of body parts, especially faces, fleeting glimpses of impersonalized people, and fragmented representations of behavior may or may not be aesthetically pleasing, but all too often they are ethnographically unsound.

Like holism itself, "whole people in whole acts" is not a dictum to be followed slavishly. It does not mean that we describe or film everything about everything. A twelve-hour camera-eye view of life in the village square would not be ethnographically effective. But the holistic principle must be kept in mind as a corrective principle for making films more ethnographic.

Another major feature of ethnography is the goal of truth. On some philosophical level it may be argued that reality cannot be truthfully represented. But for our present purposes we can usefully hold that accuracy and truth are essential to ethnography; that there are some accepted conventional distortions of reality which occur in the translation of the living act on to the printed page; and that ethnographers are fairly well aware of the conventions of distortion and are fairly well agreed on what constitutes illegitimate (by name, "dishonest" or "unscientific") distortion.

The conventions of cinematographic honesty are quite different. Cinema has developed primarily as a medium for imaginative statements in which questions of scientific-type accuracy are often irrelevant. Much of what is taught in film schools is how to translate or distort reality for aesthetic effect. These techniques include selective composition of shots, staging acted scenes, editing for continuity effect, and utilizing sound recorded in other contexts. Some of these reality-distorting techniques are inevitable in even the most scrupulously ethnographic films. But in order to judge the ethnographicness of a film we have the need to know how much and to what degree reality was distorted. And in making ethnographic films we can ask that distortions are kept to a minimum and used for ethnographic purposes, not for merely cinematographic reasons. For example, when editing *Dani Houses* and *Dani Sweet Potatoes* I could have used vaguely appropriate sound recorded two years before I shot my own footage. But I chose not to use this wild sound, or any sound other than the narration. As a result, the two films seem tedious and empty to some viewers. But I had decided, on ethnographic grounds, that the inappropriateness of the wild sound would override the viewing pleasure of audiences accustomed to more technically elaborate films.

Choices of this sort must be made deliberately, not by default. For example, when Donald and Ronald Rundstrom and Clinton Bergum were making *The Path*, they wanted to describe the flow of movement and the use of kinesic energy in the Japanese tea ceremony. In order to show this with the greatest effectiveness, they shot and edited in a way which lost the casual social gossipy nature of the tea ceremony. The film represents only one side of the reality of the ceremony. But the decisions of what to depict and what to omit were deliberate ethnographic decisions.

These, then, are the ethnographic demands for a general-use ethnographic film, that is, one which is relatively self-explanatory for casual use but which demands an accompanying written ethnography for more serious use and deeper understanding. It is difficult to imagine a film which could carry enough ethnographic contextualization and generalization to be fully self-sufficient even for serious use. At the other extreme, we are now beginning to see some films which use only synchronous sound, without any generalizing narration. Ethnographically such films can be extremely effective when used in close connection with a written ethnography or when presented by a well-prepared instructor/informant. But even though they may entirely relegate the generalizing to the written word, the degree to which these films are judged ethnographic must still depend on the degree to which they satisfy the other requirements of ethnographic film discussed above.

To define "ethnographic film" requires either one sentence or an entire book. The sentence is: "Ethnographic film is film which reflects ethnographic understanding." This book is an exploration of the nature of ethnographic film. Whatever it is, it is more than the simple sum of ethnography plus film.

It is easy to show the faults in those ethnographic films which are even less than the sum of the two: films made by an ethnographer who happens to take a movie camera into the field, or films made by a filmmaker who happens to wander among an exotic tribe. Often even such films have some documentary value, but they are inevitably missed monumental opportunities. The answer is not simply for a filmmaker to take a course or a degree in anthropology; nor is it enough for an anthropologist to enroll in film school. This is what I mean by emphasizing that ethnographic film is more than the mechanical joining of the two. The effort of thinking cinematically about ethnography or thinking ethnographically through film results in a new and different understanding of each of these disciplines. There is much good writing about how to make film and about how to do ethnography, but none of it goes far enough for our purposes here; none of it really talks about what happens to each when they are successfully blended.

Both film and ethnography involve particular ways of viewing the world.

Ethnographic film should represent the best of both ethnography and film. This can be done by respecting the constraints of each discipline and taking advantage of the opportunities and insights of each. All this is just saying, in abstract, programmatic phrases, that which the rest of this book makes explicit.

The Differing Natures of Ethnography and Film

There are profound differences between ethnography and film which are corollaries of the obvious differences between word-on-paper versus photo-on-celluloid. Having said that the differences begin with word versus picture, I will examine the consequences of it, and in particular how all this has to do with the way in which people go about the two enterprises.

The ethnographic research which culminates in a book and the filmmaking which culminates in a film are quite different enterprises which can be schematized as follows:

The Ethnographer	The Filmmaker
Begins with theoretical problems and research plans	Begins with an idea and a script
Gathers data by making observations and asking questions	Shoots footage
Analyzes data	Edits footage
Writes and rewrites	
Produces a written report	Produces a film

Cinematography makes irreversible choices at the very beginning. The finished film can only contain those images which were shot at the beginning. Especially in ethnographic filmmaking, where the shooting is done in the field and is completed before the editing begins, the editing stage is one of manipulating a finite amount of set material. Scenes can be shortened, thrown out, or their sequence juggled, and titles and narration can be added. But, practically speaking, new footage cannot be created at the editing table.

Imagine for a moment a comparable situation in ethnography: the ethnographer spends a few months in the field, writing down his observations in his notebook. Then he returns home, makes a Xerox copy of the notebook, and with scissors and paste proceeds to fashion an ethnography out of the sentences and paragraphs which he wrote down in the field. He can take sentences from different pages of the notebook and juxtapose them into new paragraphs. But he cannot write any new words or sentences.

In reality the ethnographer writes and rewrites, analyzes and reanalyzes: in short, he composes and recomposes words into sentences and sentences into paragraphs. The final ethnography hardly contains a single phrase as originally set down in the first field record. On the other hand, except for a few printed titles, the final ethnographic film contains only the images which were originally photographed. The basic difference in the way in which understanding enters the process is dramatically illustrated by the fact that when the footage has been shot, someone other than the photographer can (and usually does) edit it into the finished film, but it would be almost impossible to write an ethnography from someone else's field notes.

This difference between editing (the film) and rewriting (the book) has several implications. First, while the thorough understanding of what is going on emerges at the end of the ethnographic process, it must precede the filmmaking. Of course, the ethnographer must begin gathering data with some research plan in mind. But actually, many of the most important data are gathered on the fringe, so to speak, by means other than the preestablished research procedures. The peripheral vision of the anthropologist is often an extremely important research tool. We rarely talk about it, or systematize it, but we do use it. Also, as the anthropologist comes to understand the behavior of a people better, he can retrieve data from his own memory or from the memories of his informants. Such convenient hindsight is of no help to the cinematographer. Time past cannot be refilmed. A ceremony is filmed on the basis of whatever understanding (and luck) the filmmakers had at the moment of filming. (And I would insist that "lucky shots" are usually the rewards of understanding.) Later, when the filmmakers know more, they can film a different ceremony, and they can cut and shuffle the old footage. They can edit, but they cannot rewrite.

Ethnographic understanding emerges from the analysis, and an ethnography is only as good as the analysis. But an ethnographic film can only be as good as the understanding which precedes the filmmaking. Or, put another way, the degree to which a film is ethnographic depends on the degree to which prior ethnographic understanding has informed the filmmaking. This is the most basic message of this entire book, and I shall repeat it often in different ways.

Filmmaking is not quite so rigidly locked into first impressions as the preceding lines might suggest, but the qualifications only strengthen the argument. Often in ethnographic filmmaking, we find a wordy narration used as a bridge, or bandage, to patch over a gap in the footage, where some sequence has not been fully filmed. Usually this gap is the result of ignorance, where the cameraman has not understood well enough what was going on to be able to anticipate and to shoot satisfactory footage. The inability to anticipate meant that the camera wound down, or was unloaded at the crucial moment, or the cameraman was not even present. But it is significant, in the context of this argument, that the filmic gap is frequently closed by words. When this is done, then the filmicness of the film is diminished, and the product edges toward a spoken book. We have already insisted that ethnographic films be maximally ethnographic; but ethnographic films should also be maximally filmic.

"Truth" in Film and Ethnography

A basic problem, already mentioned in this chapter, which runs through all considerations of ethnographic film concerns the nature of truth. Filmmakers and ethnographers, when they think of it at all, take quite different positions on truth. Certainly everyone subscribes to truth. No one really advocates untruth. But filmmakers can comfortably take the artists' position that they manipulate reality through a series of falsehoods in order to create a higher truth. This appeal to higher truth has been made in more or less epigrammatic form, by all sorts of artists. Anthropologists, as scientists, assume that they must challenge the legitimacy of these facilitating lies. In science, the end cannot justify the means: results are only as sound as the methodology which produces them. Nice words. But if we look a bit more closely, we see that anthropologists have their own methodological conventions for reaching truth. And we should be rather explicit about them.

If one were to ask anthropologists to name the five best ethnographies, or the five which they liked best, one would have no trouble getting lists from most anthropologists. Actually, "five best" might be too much of an American-specific concept, and one might have to rephrase the question for anthropologists of other cultures: for example, "five really first-rate ethnographies." But lists would still be forthcoming. If one next asked the same anthropologists if truth was important to ethnography, the response would be a unanimous yes. But then if one asked for a list of the five truest, or most accurate ethnographies, there would be trouble. People would hesitate, ask for clarification, and, if they produced a list at all, it would not overlap much with their list of the "five best."

Assuming that I am correct about the thinking of my anthropological colleagues, what is going on here? One important difference between the five best and the five truest ethnographies would probably be that the "truest" were safe catalogues of trait lists, while the best were works which did not attempt any sort of exhaustive coverage. Rather, they would take a selection of data and interpret these data in a particularly enlightening and convincing manner. The truth perhaps, but certainly not the whole truth.

In short, we do not really expect any ethnography (or film) to say everything about a subject. This means that there must be selection and there must be omission. Therefore, the value of an ethnography or a film cannot be judged on the basis of whether or not it has omitted things. Rather, it must be judged on the appropriateness of what has been included and how it has been handled.

All this must seem obvious, but in actual practice it is easy to forget. For example, many anthropologists criticized Robert Gardner's film *Dead Birds* on the grounds that it showed only the men's side of Dani life. When it was pointed out that many women's activities were in fact shown, the criticism was modified to "well, he didn't show enough of the women." Gardner's more recent film, *Rivers of Sand*, concerns the role of women among the Hamar of Ethiopia, and the film is dominated by the statements of one Hamar woman. Now the criticism is reversed: Gardner doesn't present the men's side. It would be small wonder if Gardner felt frustrated by these criticisms. Underlying them is the feeling that somehow a film *should* cover everything. But that is a feeling held by anthropologists who would not make such a demand of ethnographies.

There is another convention which anthropologists accept in written ethnographies but often challenge in films. That is the common device of reconstructing an account of an event from diverse data in order to make a single, reasonable, typical, "true" account. When audiences learn that the giraffe hunt in *The Hunters* was constructed in the editing room out of scenes from several different hunts, or that the battle sequence in *Dead Birds* combined footage shot at different battles, they often feel betrayed and lose confidence in the total description of a Bushman hunt or a Dani battle.

But, in fact, a comparable construction is done in ethnography—for example, in Bronislaw Malinowski's *Argonauts of the Western Pacific* (1922). This is one of the earliest and still one of the most respected ethnographies. It would certainly appear in nearly every anthropologist's "five best ethnographies" list, discussed earlier.

The middle section of that book describes a long trading expedition undertaken by the Trobriand Islanders from their homes in Sinaketa, in the north, to Dobu, an island to the south. Now, Malinowski had not actually participated in any such expedition. His account is reconstructed from brief observations of somewhat similar events and from accounts which he gathered from his Trobriand informants. His defense of this technique is worth quoting at some length, since in so many ways Malinowski laid the foundation for ethnographic field work and is still a powerful role model for ethnographers:

> In the twelve preceding chapters, we have followed an expedition from Sinaketa to Dobu. . . . As I have seen, indeed followed, a big *uvalaku* expedition from the South to the Trobriands, I shall be able to give some of the scenes from direct impression, and not from reconstruction. Such a reconstruction for one who has seen much of the natives' tribal life and has a good grip over intelligent informants is neither very difficult nor need it be fanciful at all. Indeed, towards the end of my second visit, I had several times opportunities to check such a reconstruction by witnessing the actual occurrence, for after my first year's stay in the Trobriands I had written out already some of my material. As a rule, even in minute details, my reconstructions hardly differed from reality, as the tests have shown. None the less, it is possible for an ethnographer to enter into concrete details with more conviction when he describes things actually seen. (Malinowski 1922:376)

This sort of reconstruction of an event in written description is an accepted convention in ethnography. It is not exclusively used, of course. Malinowski himself brought in rich specific case studies, or anecdotes, as well as these generalized reconstructions. The point is that the general reconstruction, when used properly, is a legitimate ethnographic descriptive device. But there are differences between print and film uses of this convention. A good example is the housebuilding of the Dani. I have described Dani construction in print (1970:261–263) and in film (*Dani Houses*, 1974). During the years that I lived in West New Guinea with the Dani, I observed housebuilding many times but I never saw all the steps in building any one house. I formed a complete picture of Dani construction from countless isolated observations of Dani at work. I am now somewhat embarrassed to realize that I never actually wrote these qualifications in my ethnography. And my account is phrased in very general terms. It begins: "The main part of the construction is done by the men and boys who will live in the men's house. Chopping of lumber and actual construction is done only by men; women carry wood and thatch grass to the site . . ." (1970:261).

I did not tell the reader where I got my information. But presumably most readers would understand this as a general account. And, in contrast, when I later discussed "magic associated with housebuilding," I was very careful not to claim these data as general, saying: "At Anisimo a knot of grass. . . . At Biem, dried banana leaf was wrapped around the base. . . . At Musanima . . . [these are all names of specific compound sites]" (1970:263).

In the film *Dani Houses*, I used footage of that instance of banana leaf magic mentioned in this quotation. However, while in the book it is clear that I only observed that banana leaf magic once, there is no way for the film viewer to know this. And in fact, most viewers would probably assume that such banana leaf magic was a standard part of Dani housebuilding. On the surface this is a minor ethnographic detail, but such situations are multiplied many times in the course of any ethnographic film, and the problem of truth becomes a major consideration.

Also, while shooting the film *Dani Houses*, I had missed several steps in the sequences. But during the editing I made the decision not to edit diverse shots together for continuity, but rather to keep them separate, in the order in which they had occurred. For example, the first sequence in the film follows the construction of two pig sties. I had footage of women carrying the thatch grass to the construction site, but I did not get footage of the grass being plucked. For a later sequence, there is footage of both the plucking and the carrying to the site of a round house. I decided to use the plucking footage in the second sequence, where it belonged. But that means that we first see thatch grass appear without knowing how it was gathered. It would have made for a smoother, more logical film to have used the plucking footage in the first sequence. But since it was of different people in a different place I held out for accuracy.

There was yet another dilemma in *Dani Houses*. I had filmed half the construction of a men's round house and then, through some circumstances not relevant to the housebuilding itself, I missed the completion of that house. Later I filmed the second half of the construction of a women's round house. It would have been possible, by choosing proper shooting angles, and through clever editing, to present the two houses as one. Instead I deliberately emphasized that they were separate and mentioned the differences between men's and women's houses.

These sorts of specific, demystifying approaches are becoming more common in ethnography as well as in ethnographic film. We have seen that

Malinowski, writing in the 1920s and 1930s, used both the specific illustration and the generalized description. My own monograph is somewhat more generalizing then Malinowski's works, while my films (finished several years later) represent more uncompromising specifics. Of course, words lend themselves to generalizing statements more easily than does film, while the specificity of the film image makes filmic generalizations less satisfactory and more manipulative.

In written accounts we usually have some idea of the extent to which a description is specific, reconstructed, or generalized. Choice of verb form, use of parenthetical expressions, footnotes, explanatory paragraphs, all offer opportunities to qualify or support written data. We usually do not get comparable information in films. It is more difficult to slip in parenthetical information in a film. When a description must be seen from beginning to end at a predetermined speed, without pause or backtracking, there is no place for a footnote. Of course, it would still be possible to include qualifying information in a film, but it would be more intrusive and the conventions of filmmaking are against it.

Chapter 2

A History of Ethnographic Film

Santayana's famous dictum that "those who cannot remember the past are condemned to repeat it" may make for bad politics, as the historian David Hackett Fischer argues (1970:157), but it is a good rule for science. In science—and we may include ethnographic film here—those who do not understand the achievements of the past may be lucky enough to reinvent them. Unfortunately, the history of ethnographic film has been a fifty-year tale of failure to appreciate the past and, too often, even failure to reinvent its accomplishments.

This chapter is a very selective historical sketch of the development of ethnographic film, intended to show what was learned, as well as what has been allowed to slip from our awareness, in the five decades since *Nanook of the North*. It is based on those films which I happened to have been able to see and study in the United States through 1974. And it is a historical prologue to the next chapter. We can still hope for a definitive (or at least a comprehensive) history of ethnographic film.

The history of ethnographic film is one part of the history of cinematography itself, and more particularly of documentary, or nonfiction film. Both film and ethnography were born in the nineteenth century and reached their maturity in the 1920s. But curiously enough, it was not until the 1960s that film and ethnography systematically began to join in effective collaboration. The few earlier exceptions had little impact on either film or ethnography. And even this later development has occurred only in the United States, France, Australia, and, to a much lesser degree, Great Britain. Again, curiously, such countries as Japan, India, and Sweden, which have both thriving film industries and solid academic anthropology, have made no important contribution to ethnographic film. Even Germany, despite the encouragement of the Encyclopaedia Cinematographica archive in Göttingen, did not contribute substantially to this development.

However, we shall see that, during the first forty years of ethnographic film, the major contributions were made by people who were outside (or uncomfortably on the fringe of) the film industry and others who were more or less peripheral to anthropology.

Background Factors

Before diving into the history of ethnographic film, we should at least mention several factors which lie behind its development, namely, cinema technology, the economics of filmmaking, and the development of ethnography.

DEVELOPMENT OF TECHNOLOGY

By the beginning of the twentieth century, the basic cinema technology which was a prerequisite to ethnographic film was available. By the mid-1960s, synchronous sound-film equipment was portable enough and reliable enough to be used in even the most remote regions. And by 1970, we had fully portable videotape equipment. The first development was, of course, essential to any ethnographic filming; the second development, lightweight synchronous sound equipment, allowed simultaneous recording of the visual and aural aspects of an event. This created an important new dimension of reality and allowed the filmmaker to avoid the pitfalls of narration and postsynchronized background sounds. But the synchronous sound equipment is expensive and requires a team: minimally, one person to operate the camera and another to run the tape recorder.

The third development, videotape, has the great advantage of instant playback with synchronous sound. And videotape's capacity for making long takes without stopping to rewind or reload should allow cameramen to be able to capture important moments of spontaneous behavior, now so much a matter of luck with a movie camera. But videotape is still too expensive, too unreliable, and of too low quality to have been used much in the field.

ECONOMICS

Film is expensive. It is expensive to shoot footage, to complete a film, to distribute the film, and to rent or buy it for viewing. (Chapter four, on making ethnographic films, goes into more details on expenses.) Until the 1960s, ethnographers had little assurance that the film would even be distributed. Practically no ethnographic films have been successful on commercial markets, and on the educational market only a very few films make back their costs. Until recently, anthropology departments of colleges and universities, now the main market for ethnographic films, rarely could afford to rent or buy films for teaching. Research budgets were minuscule. Most research expeditions in the 1920s and 1930s cost only a few hundred dollars in hard cash from initial proposal to published monograph. Academic salaries were low. It was not until the 1960s that relative affluence reached both individuals and institutions in the academic world. The great increase in ethnographic filmmaking during the 1960s was probably due more to the improved economic conditions of individuals, funding agencies, and departmental budgets than to any purely intellectual causes.

THE DEVELOPMENT OF ETHNOGRAPHY

The 1920s saw the firm establishment of fieldwork-based ethnography and the responsible popularization of ethnographic insights. Many important ethnographic monographs had been published earlier, but 1922 was a landmark year: then both A. R. Radcliffe-Brown's *Andaman Islanders* and Bronislaw Malinowski's *Argonauts of the Western Pacific* were published. These men were to dominate British anthropology for the next two decades. Malinowski wrote several more monographs on the Trobriand Islanders. His books had provocative titles (e.g., *The Sexual Life of Savages*) and an easy style, and they were read far beyond the borders of academic anthropology. In the United States, the gap between academic and popular was being bridged even more successfully by Margaret Mead and later Ruth Benedict.

Mead had carried out research in Samoa in 1925–1926. Her monograph *Social Organization of Manua* (1930a) was written for her colleagues, but in *Coming of Age in Samoa* (1928) she had attempted to make her Samoan data relevant to current United States concerns. In her later work in New Guinea, Mead followed the same pattern: technical monographs for the profession, and relevant ethnographies for the public, addressed to problems like child rearing, education, and sex roles. Then, in 1934, came Ruth Benedict's *Patterns of Culture*, which further synthesized and popularized anthropology.

Certainly, Mead had established the validity of popular professional ethnography which could encompass both solid scientific research and responsible popularization. But there was no attempt in that decade by anthropologists to use film for comparable purposes.

For reasons of geographical accident at least, Robert Flaherty's first two films should have been of particular personal interest to American anthropologists. *Nanook* was made on the eastern shore of the Hudson Bay, some 700 miles south of Baffin Island, where Franz Boas, the dominant figure in American anthropology, had spent a year in 1883–1884. Although by 1922, when *Nanook* was finished, Boas had become primarily concerned with Northwest Coast Indians, he must have had continuing interest in

Eskimos. And Flaherty made his second film, *Moana*, on Savai'i, in Western Samoa, less than 300 miles from Manua, in Eastern Samoa, where Margaret Mead, who had been one of Boas's students, did her fieldwork. *Moana* was first shown in New York in 1926, while Mead was in Samoa, and she had heard of the film even while she was in the field (see Mead 1972:154). It is hard to imagine that Flaherty's films were not seen by anthropologists. But if Boas, Mead, and the other American anthropologists even saw Flaherty's films, there is no indication that they appreciated their ethnographic implications. (However, as we shall see, Mead did play a major role in the development of ethnographic film in the late 1930s, and maybe a lag of only a decade shouldn't be surprising. But if she, or anyone else, was inspired by Flaherty's films, they did not mention it in print.)

In short, despite the availability of cinema technology since the turn of the century, despite the popular models since the 1920s, and perhaps because of financial problems before the 1960s, anthropology did not contribute to ethnographic film in any systematic way during the early decades.

From the vantage point of the 1970s, the history of the four decades from *Nanook* to *Dead Birds* is marked by only a few real achievements in ethnographic film. A good deal of footage was shot. Some of this is preserved in the German archives, and more will be preserved in the National Anthropological Film Center in Washington, now in the planning stage. But in this casual history we need mention only a few great achievements. They are the films of Robert Flaherty, beginning with *Nanook* in 1922; *Grass* (1925) by Merian C. Cooper and Ernest B. Schoedsack; the scripted films of the late 1920s and early 1930s; the Balinese films of Bateson and Mead, shot in the 1930s and released in the 1950s; Jean Rouch's films of the late 1950s; John Marshall's *The Hunters* of 1956; and Robert Gardner's *Dead Birds* in 1963.

Pre-1922

It is always satisfying to have some definite date with which to begin a history. For ethnographic film, Jean Rouch (1970:13) suggests that it should be 4 April 1901. On that day Baldwin Spencer, who was to become famous for his studies of the Australian aborigines, shot footage of an aborigine kangaroo dance and a rain ceremony. The few other ethnographic films, or films on tribal peoples, which were made before 1922 may be mentioned in passing (see O'Reilly 1970). The Hamburg South Sea Expedition of 1908–

1910 made a twenty-minute film on various topics, especially dances, in Micronesia and Melanesia. In 1912, Gaston Melies, brother of the important cinema pioneer Georges, made some short films of the sort which Patrick O'Reilly calls "documentaires romances" in Tahiti and New Zealand (1970). In 1914 Edward Curtis, famous for his sensitive romantic photographic portraits of American Indians, made a scripted epic of the Kwakiutl Indians, which has recently been restored and rereleased under the title *In the Land of the War Canoes*. And in 1917 and 1918, Martin and Osa Johnson shot some travel films of cannibal life in the Solomon Islands and the New Hebrides of the Western Pacific.

Robert Flaherty

If ethnographic film was conceived in 1901 when Baldwin Spencer shot his first footage of Australian aborigines, it was born on 11 June 1922, when Robert Flaherty's Eskimo film, *Nanook of the North*, opened in a New York theater. The film became an immediate success and was seen by audiences around the world. But *Nanook*'s success was singular. It did not really open the doors for ethnographic film, or even for Robert Flaherty. He had great problems financing new film projects. *Nanook* has always been a great landmark. When I took introductory anthropology courses at Harvard in the years before *The Hunters* was released, *Nanook* and Flaherty's other ethnographic films, *Moana* and *Man of Aran*, were practically the only films used in anthropology courses. In the 1970s, with dozens of ethnographic films available, *Nanook* and *Moana* are still favorites.

Many details of Flaherty's life are cloaked in the myths which he spun about them during his lifetime and which his admirers repeated after his death. One approaches him through his two biographies (Griffith 1953; Calder-Marshall 1963), with a mixture of confusion and amusement. But myths aside, his accomplishments were real.

Flaherty was a mining engineer and explorer. Like Boas, the physicist, in Baffinland, and Alfred Haddon, the marine biologist, in the Torres Strait, he went to the field in the interests of a traditional science and found his attention turned from the things of sea and land to the people who lived there. He lived in Eskimo country and traveled with Eskimos for long periods between 1910 and 1921. In 1914 he shot his first Eskimo footage, but it was destroyed in a fire. The Flaherty legend tells of a careless cigarette which ignited the highly flammable nitrate-base film stock. Arthur Calder-Marshall (1963:74) is probably right in his assessment of the incident: it saved Flaherty from trying to sell an amateurish film, and it sent him back to film *Nanook*. Returning to Hudson Bay, he shot the footage for *Nanook* in 1921–1922, and it was finished in the summer of 1922. The next year he went to Samoa to try to repeat the success of *Nanook*. His Samoan film, *Moana* (subtitled: *A Romance of the Golden Age*), was released in 1926, but it never had the phenomenal commercial success of *Nanook*. During the next years he made two more trips to Polynesia to assist other directors in fictional romances but each time withdrew from the project before the film was finished. Flaherty shot his third major film on the Aran Islands, off the west coast of Ireland, between 1931 and 1933, and *Man of Aran* was released in 1934. In 1935 he again ventured into purely commercial film-making—this time *Elephant Boy*, in India. Flaherty stayed with this film to the end, but his contributions were finally overwhelmed by the producer and the result was not a "Flaherty film." In 1939–1941 he made *The Land* under U.S. government contract, about the American agricultural depression. But *The Land* raised great political opposition and has never been widely distributed. His last film, *Louisiana Story*, shot in 1946–1948, was released in 1948, and, at the time of his death in 1951, he was planning a film on Hawaii.

It is clear that Flaherty's accomplishments were achieved at tremendous personal cost. He tried to function in the world of commercial film, but his films were too ethnographic for that, and his ethnography was too naïve and self-invented to give him access to academia. But, even though Flaherty had little effect on later ethnographic films, there are several aspects of his approach which should be recognized.

INTENSIVE IMMERSION

Although Flaherty was no ethnographer and did not pretend to approach cultures with an ethnographic research plan, he did spend an extended time in the field for each film, observing and absorbing the native culture. He was no fly-by-night explorer. He lived in Eskimo country for much of 11 years (about 12 months while shooting *Nanook*), in Samoa for 1¾ years, Ireland for 1½ years, and over one year in the Louisiana bayous. His commitment to something like the ethnographic technique of personal immersion in a culture was remarkable. Frances Flaherty's description of how they went about making *Moana* (Griffith 1953:52–71) is similar to a description of an ethnographic field trip. The Flahertys were not just living in Samoa, they were constantly searching, looking, and trying to understand Samoan life. Although length of stay does not guarantee depth of knowledge, it is a fairly essential precondition. Fleeting visits and shallow knowledge are all too evident in many later ethnographic films.

THE DRAMA OF THE SPECIFIC INDIVIDUAL: WHOLE PEOPLE

Flaherty understood the implications of film as specific, contrasted with the printed word as general. He used his films to make generalizations by following the specific acts of a specific individual: he made films which focused on Nanook, the Eskimo man; on Moana, the Samoan youth; and on the Man of Aran. He tried to do more than just give us faceless unidentified Eskimos or Samoans or Irishmen. He pushed film to its filmic specific limit, letting the audience enjoy and identify with a real, albeit exotic, individual. This may be Flaherty's most important contribution to ethnographic film, and its influence is clear in *The Hunters* and *Dead Birds*. It is safe to say that no ethnographic film has suffered from focusing too much on an individual and many are flawed by not doing so.

Flaherty tried to tell a story: not, like novels or scripted film, a story of human interaction or passion, of the search for love or wealth or power, but a story of the individual facing crisis. In *Nanook* it was man's struggle with nature; in Samoa, where nature was too beneficent, it was Moana against his culture, bearing the pain of the tattooing process which would make him a man; and in Ireland it was again man against nature, the Man of Aran against the sea.

RECONSTRUCTION AND THE ETHNOGRAPHIC PRESENT

Flaherty ventured into one of the more treacherous realms of ethnography. He created artifice to assert a truth. He convinced the Samoan youth to undergo a tattooing ceremony which had nearly died out; he persuaded the Aran Islanders to recreate their hunt for the basking sharks, a skill which they had not practiced for a generation or more. In order to film Eskimo life inside an igloo he had the Eskimo build an igloo set; it was a half-dome, twice life-size. In fact, very little of his final footage was of spontaneous behavior. The validity of these filmic distortions and their relationship to the accepted distortion of written ethnography are at the crux of the major criticism of Flaherty's ethnographic films. His films are obviously attractive and interesting, but are they true? Flaherty met this issue head-on. Calder-

Marshall quotes him as saying, "Sometimes you have to lie. One often has to distort a thing to catch its true spirit" (1963:97). We will consider this question and its implications in the next chapter.

NATIVE FEEDBACK

The Flaherty legend relates how Flaherty developed his footage each evening and screened it for his subjects, getting their reactions and advice and thus making them real collaborators in the filmmaking process. This is a fascinating idea. It has the potentially great advantage of making film more truly reflective of the natives' insight into their own culture. Unfortunately, it is not at all clear to what extent Flaherty actually did this. The one anecdote tells of the Eskimos' excited participation as they watched footage of Nanook spearing a walrus (Griffith 1953:40,41; Calder-Marshall 1963:81,82). But from this anecdote it seems only that Flaherty showed the walrus rushes as an amusing lark. There is no hint that this was the "deliberate part of a philosophy of filmmaking," as Calder-Marshall claims (1963:82). Whatever the reality, the myth is powerful. Certainly Flaherty can be credited with the very important idea of using the subjects in this way. Many ethnographic filmmakers since Flaherty have thought about making this sort of collaboration, and some have shown their completed films to their subjects. But we know little more about the potentials of this approach than we did fifty years ago. Now the idea of native feedback is in the air, and one can only hope that Flaherty's inspiration will soon bear fruit.

Another sort of native feedback came out of Flaherty's stay in Ireland. Pat Mullen, the Aran Islander who was Flaherty's "contact man" during the filming and appeared in the film, wrote a book about his experiences with Flaherty. It was called, like the film, *Man of Aran* (1935). This book was a unique document in ethnographic film. Indeed, never before or since has an informant written a book about his ethnographer. It is only matched by a recent book by Pat Loud (1974) describing her experiences as the mother and wife of "An American Family," the twelve-part television documentary produced by Craig Gilbert for National Educational Television.

VISUAL SUSPENSE

In the 1920s, of course, Flaherty was limited to silent film. He could, and did, occasionally stop the visual film to insert a printed title, but he was spared by his time from the temptation to overnarrate. Thus, he was forced to think visually. Also, to the extent that he screened rushes while in the field, he knew what he had on film and could do additional shooting immediately. He did not have to bridge over missing shots with narration.

One of Flaherty's most successful visual techniques was to follow an exotic act visually, showing it step by step as it developed, not explaining it in words. In one sequence of *Nanook* we see Nanook tugging on a line leading into a hole in the ice. We are engaged in that act, and think about it. Eventually, the suspense is broken: our questions are answered when Nanook pulls out a seal. Flaherty creates the same visual involvement when Nanook makes the igloo—especially at the end of the sequence, when Nanook cuts a slab of ice for a window, sets it in place, and fixes a snow slab reflector along one side. For a time we are puzzled and therefore involved. But when Nanook steps back, finished, we understand.

Flaherty also used this technique in *Moana* in the sequences of snaring the wild pig and smoking the robber crab out of the rocks. In both sequences, we are told that there is a Something to be caught, we see the technology involved, and finally we see the catch. In fact, the robber crab sequence has a mystery within a mystery. As the boy sets about to catch the Something, he kindles a fire by rubbing a small stick along a groove cut into a larger branch. For viewers who are not familiar with this device, called a fire plow in the ethnographic literature, the mystery is resolved only when the boy blows the embers into flame.

In this way, as Calder-Marshall points out (1963:95), Flaherty makes demands on his audience: he demands that they join him in observing the Eskimo. It is very revealing to compare the 1922 version of *Nanook* with a later one, released in 1947, four years before Flaherty's death. Now the film has been speeded up by 50 percent, from sixteen frames per second to twenty-four frames per second to accommodate sound. Where the titles with their few sparse words once were, the scenes now fade out to black and fade in to the next sequence; worse, we are subjected to a steady narration, backed by orchestral music and sounds of wind howling and dogs barking. The narration adds little information, but the steady barrage of words anticipates needlessly and comments gratuitously. In the original version, we participated in Nanook's window and admired its ingenuity; now the narrator tells us how ingenious it is and what a skilled person Nanook is. There is the great irony: one must assume that Flaherty himself collaborated in, or at least assented to, the speeded-up sound version.

Grass

Robert Flaherty dominates the ethnographic film of the 1920s on the grounds not only of the quality of his films but also the insight of his approach. But one cannot discuss the 1920s without considering the film *Grass*, shot by Merian C. Cooper and Ernest B. Schoedsack in 1924 and released in 1925. Cooper and Schoedsack had earlier shot footage in Ethiopia for a film about Haile Selassie, but, in a curious echo of Flaherty's experience with his first Eskimo film, their undeveloped negative was destroyed by a ship fire (Behlmer 1966:19). Like Flaherty, they were not diverted from filmmaking, and in 1924 they went to the Near East to make a film about exploration. They wandered around, shooting superficial travelogue footage until they reached Persia, where they joined the Bakhtiari herdsmen on their annual trek from winter to summer pastures. This is a nomadiclike pattern which is called transhumance. Cooper and Schoedsack's approach had little of the sophistication of Flaherty's. They apparently spent only a couple of months with the Bakhtiari and only peripherally focused on individuals—the Khan and his son. (Behlmer, who interviewed Cooper [1966], states that they had planned to make a second migration with the Bakhtiari, this time to film a single family, but that they ran short of funds and finished the film with only the more general footage of the first trip.)

Most of the film follows the remarkable movement of hundreds of people and thousands of animals across a wide icy river and over a steep snowy mountain range. This is in no sense a reconstruction, dependent on the filmmakers' understanding. They were obviously permitted to participate in the Bakhtiari's march and to film what they could. Neither Flaherty nor any later filmmaker ever found a man-against-nature drama which could match this in terms of sheer visual spectacle. What begins as a routine travel film becomes almost by accident an unsurpassed spontaneous drama. The film now seems dated because the intertitles are too often merely cute. And we learn little of the cultural background of the Bakhtiari. Even the book which Cooper wrote (1925) is more about the adventure than the Bakhtiari. Indeed, anticipating that the single trek will verge on the unbelievable, the film opens with a photograph of a statement notarized by the American consul in Shiraz stating that they did make the trek. We are not even told that this is a yearly migration. It is almost as if our credulity has been strained by seeing it even once. But despite its many faults as ethnography, *Grass* remains a classic bit of ethnographic data.

Scripted Fictional Films

In the late 1920s and early 1930s a number of films were shot in exotic locations, using local people to act out written fictional scripts with strong plot lines. This was a logical step beyond Flaherty's directed reconstructions in Canada, Samoa, and Ireland. In another sense, it was a logical step from the commercial films which then, as now, used natives (of Europe or the United States) to act out fictional themes from their own cultures. The "Hollywood film" was and is the epitome of this approach.

These early films were commercial ventures, taking advantage of the public interest which had been stimulated by filmmakers like Flaherty and ethnographers like Mead. But because the actors could be controlled by directors and script, these films could be made without the risks and uncertainties of documentary film. Flaherty himself became involved in this. In 1927 he went to Tahiti with W. S. Van Dyke to film *White Shadows in the South Seas* (1928). But the two men apparently could not work together, and Flaherty withdrew. The next year he returned to French Polynesia with the famous German director F. W. Murnau to make *Tabu* (1931), and again there were problems and Flaherty left. The stories of personal friction during these two ventures make good movie gossip. But it is more interesting to look at the differences between these two scripted films, which Flaherty rejected, and the films which Flaherty did on his own. *Nanook*, *Moana*, and *Man of Aran* all show untouched, untroubled cultures. In *Nanook*, the brief scenes at the fur trading post are used for benign humor and to satisfy the fur company which paid for the film. (We see Nanook listening in wonderment to a phonograph, and he tests a record with his teeth in a scene which always draws a laugh.) There is no consideration of how the intrusion of fur traders and all their cultural baggage may have affected the Eskimo.

But while Flaherty pictures the brave-and-noble-savage in the Arctic, Samoa, and Ireland, the Polynesian films of Van Dyke and Murnau show the noble-savage-corrupted-by-civilization. In fact, in *Tabu* everyone gets into the act: a weak French colonial officer, a European trader, a dishonest Chinese saloon keeper, and a relentless Polynesian chief all conspire to thwart the love of the young Polynesian couple. In both sorts of films the use of idealized cultural stereotypes, positive as well as negative, strongly reflects the romanticism of that period. It is interesting that audiences of the 1970s find Flaherty's films more palatable than the Polynesian films. But actually the Van Dyke and Murnau films should be more appealing to anthropologists because they at least allude to real sorts of problems in real sorts of situations. Modern anthropology is much more concerned with the cultural conflicts of *Tabu* than with the reconstructed initiation ceremony of *Moana*.

Cooper and Schoedsack followed *Grass* with a film made in northern Thailand called *Chang* (1927), but, ironically, the most famous scene in the film was the unscripted rampage of a wild elephant through a settlement. Cooper considered *Chang* "our best film" (personal letter to me, 1966). Later Schoedsack alone made a film called *Rango* (1931) in Sumatra, starring an orangutan. Cooper and Schoedsack went one more step into fantasy to make *King Kong* (1933), shot in Hollywood back lots and studios, but set on an island off Java, with the "natives" speaking bits of Swahili and Malay, wielding shields of vague New Guinea derivation and chasing a gorillalike ape.

Knud Rasmussen, the Danish-Eskimo explorer and ethnographer, collaborated in *Wedding of Palo* (1937), shot in eastern Greenland. Palo's story seems at first suspiciously Hollywood, but in fact appears to be based on a traditional Eskimo love story. Another film called simply *Eskimo* treats an Eskimo love story disrupted by the captain of a trading vessel frozen in the ice near a village. This tradition continues on in the United States with such recent films as the 1974 Eskimo story *White Dawn*. It has produced masterpieces of what might be called ethnographic fiction like Satyajit Ray's *World of Apu* trilogy (*Pather Panchali*, 1955; *The Unvanquished*, 1957; and *The World of Apu*, 1959), which follows Apu and his family from boyhood in a Bengal village to university life in Calcutta (see Wood 1971); or the Algerian-French production *Ramparts of Clay* (1969), based on Jean Duvignaud's monograph on a Tunisian village, *Change at Shebika* (1970).

The major strength of the ethnographic fiction film is its ability to focus on peak events of interpersonal relationships and so to explore in detail the dynamics of emotions as they are played out. The danger is that the cultural context may be ethnocentric and shallow. It is a great gamble which is rarely attempted and even more rarely won. But the best of the ethnographic fiction films, those which are true to the culture, bring to focus the question which we have already touched on: Can fiction create truth? In the next chapter we shall return to this question.

Bateson and Mead in Bali and New Guinea

A decade after Flaherty's first films, ethnography and film were finally brought together by two anthropologists, Gregory Bateson and Margaret Mead. Bateson had done fieldwork among the Iatmul of the Sepik River in northeastern New Guinea and had written a monograph, *Naven* (1936), a complex book with a theoretical sophistication of analysis which has made it a much-admired but little-read masterpiece. Mead had done fieldwork in Samoa and New Guinea, had written numerous monographs and articles, and was already well known for her readable popular ethnographies: *Coming of Age in Samoa*, 1928; *Growing Up in New Guinea*, 1930b; and *Sex and Temperament in Three Primitive Societies*, 1935. Then between 1936 and 1939, Bateson and Mead collaborated in a joint study of a Balinese village. The Balinese project made several major contributions to anthropology, but the one which concerns us here was the integration of film and still photography into ethnographic research. As they wrote in 1942 (p. xii), they used photographs to cover some of the criticisms of their separate earlier work—as a visual filling out of Bateson's impersonalized abstraction, and as verifiable documentation for Mead's broad impressionistic descriptions of human behavior. Their research in Bali covered many subjects and was carried out in collaboration with Jane Belo, Colin McPhee, and others then working in Bali. But the focus of Bateson and Mead's research was on the relationship of culture and personality, and particularly on child rearing, which had already been an important theme in Mead's earlier work.

The first book to be published, *Balinese Character* (Bateson and Mead 1942), used a combination of text and still photographs in a way which has rarely been attempted since and has never been surpassed. The movie footage seems to have been less important, or perhaps simply more difficult to shoot, than the still photographs. In any case, Bateson and Mead eventually used the stills in their major publication on Bali (1942), while the films were only finished a decade later under the supervision of Mead alone. The entire project warrants much more consideration and thought than it has received.

But here I want to talk only about the films. In addition to the 25,000 still photographs which were culled for the two Bali books, (Bateson and Mead 1942; Mead and MacGregor 1951), Bateson shot 22,000 feet of 16-mm. movie film. From this, six films were edited and released in 1950. These films are ethnographic in the most literal sense of the word. Like written ethnographies, they describe behavior and present the results of the ethnographic study. For the most part, they focus on children interacting with each other and with adults. For example, they try to show visually the Balinese practice of stimulating an infant nearly to the point of climax and then suddenly breaking off contact. This pattern is important in contributing to the nonclimaxing "steady state" of adult Balinese, and it has visual manifestations which can be shown well in film.

Two features of the Bateson and Mead series are particularly noteworthy. One film is a longitudinal study of a single boy, Karba, from seven months to thirty-four months of age, following him through the crucial developmental stages of early childhood. In *Childhood Rivalry in Bali and New Guinea*, the Balinese behavior is set off against the very different behavior of a different culture, the Iatmul, whom Bateson had studied between 1929 and 1933, and whom they revisited for eight months in the middle of their Balinese research.

The Bateson and Mead research was the first to try systematically to work out the implications of using film as an integral part of anthropological research and reportage, a problem treated in most of the next chapter. In a written ethnography, it seems easy (because we are accustomed to do so) to use words to describe critical moments and practices, to describe the development of a child through phases, and to set the behavior of a particular culture into a cross-cultural context. Bateson and Mead did this in print, of course. They also used film, not to do just the same thing, but toward the same ends. They deliberately used film to show visual movement and holistic interrelationships of complex scenes which could be much better presented on film than described purely in words. Thus, their use of film was planned to be integrated fully with, and supplementary to, the written ethnography.

Another major contribution was Bateson and Mead's concern with spelling out the circumstances of their photography. In the book *Balinese Character* (1942), Bateson has contributed a chapter (pp. 49–54) in which he explicitly discusses the question of Balinese camera consciousness and suggests factors which diminish its influence; distinguishes between posed photographs and photographs taken in contexts which the anthropologists created, for example, by paying for a dance; describes the various sorts of selections in the original shooting and final editing; mentions the matter of retouching photographs; and explains various technological factors. Elsewhere, Mead (1970) has emphasized the importance of laying out these same basic facts. But on the whole, even this minimal prerequisite for scientific credibility has not been repeated.

There are problems in the Balinese films. Some are purely technical. In the 1930s, Bateson was limited to clumsy, tripod camera without synchronous sound, and to relatively short takes. And because of financial concern, he shot most of his footage at 16 frames per second (f.p.s.). When the film was edited, it included Mead's narration and was intended to be projected at 24 instead of 16 f.p.s. The irony is obvious. This ethnographic report, which is so concerned with natural movement and pace of life, shows the Balinese moving at a pace 50 percent faster than normal. (It seems to be a matter of faith among film people that the faster speed—"sound speed"—is essential to high quality sound. In fact, if the Balinese films are projected at the speed at which they were shot, 16 f.p.s., Mead's voice drops an octave or so but is still understandable, and the Balinese pace can be appreciated. However, this is not always feasible. Some modern projectors do not have 16-f.p.s. capability or an automatic sound switch-off at that speed.) Fortunately, most of the footage used in *Trance and Dance in Bali* seems to have been shot originally at 24 f.p.s.

A more serious problem in the Balinese films is that the action on the screen often does not show clearly what the narration claims. This may be in part a result of the way the footage was originally conceived. It is not really clear to what extent the footage was intended to illustrate the ethnographic understandings. Neither ethnographer has written much about this aspect of their research. But in one passage Bateson writes that "we treated the cameras in the field as recording instruments, not as devices for illustrating our theses" (Bateson and Mead 1942:49). This is rather ambiguous. The final ethnographic reports, like the films, were written to prove their theses. That is, selections from the data and from the footage were made, and the final results were interpretive. And I certainly would not now want to defend the position that "objective" footage is desirable, or even possible. I under-stand it to mean that, since the footage was shot as the research proceeded, some understandings of Balinese culture were reached only when it was too late to capture them on film.

The Bateson and Mead ethnographic films represent a major advance in concept, even if that concept could not be fully realized. But, like Flaherty, they have had little real effect. It is frustrating to speculate how much more advanced ethnographic films might now be if the Bateson and Mead innova-tions in the visual field had been widely understood and built on in the 1940s and 1950s.

Marshall, Gardner, Asch, and Others: Developments at Harvard

For the two decades after Bateson and Mead's Balinese expedition, the ethnographic film scene was quiescent. The Second World War had inter-vened, of course, diverting personnel and resources and closing down field opportunities. It was not until the 1950s that ethnographic film began to flourish again. When it did, an extraordinary amount of the crucial activity was based in and around Harvard University and was carried out by a few men who had all worked together at one time or another.

What might be called the Harvard movement really started outside aca-demia with the Marshall family expeditions to the Kalahari Bushmen. Beginning in 1951, Laurence K. Marshall, a retired businessman, led a series of expeditions into the Kalahari Desert of southern Africa to study the Bushmen. Although the Marshall expeditions included scientists of various sorts, their core was always Marshall and his family: his wife, Lorna, and his two children, Elizabeth and John. It was planned that Mrs. Marshall would make ethnographic studies of the Bushmen, John would make films, and Elizabeth, who had a flair for writing, would write a book. Fortunately no anthropologist was around to tell them how unfeasible it all was. The results were outstanding. George Peter Murdock has referred to "ethnographic accounts of outstanding quality . . . by . . . housewives like Lorna Marshall" (1972:18). Elizabeth Marshall Thomas's book *The Harmless People* (1959) has become a classic popular account, and John Marshall's films have played a major role in the development of ethnographic film.

By 1954 John Marshall had shot hundreds of thousands of feet of film on the Bushmen. About this time, the Marshalls contacted J. O. Brew, then director of the Peabody Museum at Harvard. Brew recognized the value of the Marshall footage and invited the family to collaborate with Harvard. The Film Study Center was established in the basement of the Peabody Museum, and a graduate student in the anthropology department at Harvard, Robert Gardner, was chosen to be its director. Gardner had just passed his graduate orals and had a solid background in film as well as anthropology. In the early 1950s, while he was a graduate student in anthropology at the University of Washington, he had founded and run a small documentary film company called Orbit Films. Orbit produced two ethnographic films on the Kwakiutl of British Columbia, called *Blunden Harbor* and *Dances of the Kwakiutl*. When he was at Harvard with the Film Study Center, Gardner returned to ethnographic film. He accompanied the Marshalls to the Kalahari in 1955 and then helped John Marshall edit a portion of the Bushman footage into a film called *The Hunters*.

THE HUNTERS

The Hunters was finished in 1956 and released in 1958. It quickly became a most popular and respected ethnographic film. In many ways it was pure Flaherty. Based on long but nonprofessional study of a people, it followed four individuals through a major man-against-nature crisis, the hunt for meat, which culminated in the killing of a giraffe.

The film can be criticized on a number of grounds. It tells a story, but a story which was composed in the editing room with footage shot not over a single two-week period but on expeditions which took place over several years. There are some inconsistencies which bother the fastidious viewer: the four hunters are not always the same people; stock giraffe footage is edited in omnisciently while the hunters are still searching for it. (However, the persistent rumor that the giraffe was finished off with a rifle is not true.)

The most serious problem with *The Hunters* today is that its basic premise is inaccurate, as John Marshall is the first to recognize now. In the mid-fifties, when the film was made, the best anthropological opinion held that hunting and gathering groups like the Bushmen were hanging on to a marginal environment with an inadequate subsistence technology. This was at least partially the result of the way fieldwork had been done. For example, the Marshall expedition, appearing in a Bushman camp with its trucks loaded with food and water (Thomas 1959:5–6), certainly must have tempted the Bushmen to exaggerate their subsistence problems. And there would have been little reason for the Marshalls to doubt what they were told by both Bushmen and anthropologists. In the early 1960s, anthropologists like Richard Lee worked among hunters and gatherers, accompanying the people without the benefit of Land Rover and masses of supplies, making careful studies of what the Bushmen actually ate. Lee showed that the Bushmen actually had an abundance of food—especially in the undramatic but protein-packed mongongo nuts which were available by the millions. Equally careful ethnography elsewhere contributed to revised versions of other foraging groups. The publication of *Man the Hunter* (Lee and De Vore 1968) marked the acceptance of a new understanding of hunting and gathering peoples. It also meant that the major premise of *The Hunters* (that the Bushmen were starving) could no longer be accepted. But, although the film is ethnographically faulty on the role of hunting in Bushman life, its portrayal of the hunting itself remains unimpeached. (In this connection, it is worth noting that Marshall's 1958 essay on Bushman hunting has been reprinted in the most recent collection of readings on African anthropology [Skinner 1972]).

The Hunters did not really represent a conceptual advance beyond Flaherty or Bateson and Mead. As a film, it was better than Flaherty's. The account of Bushman hunting was more systematic, and throughout the narration Marshall tried to penetrate the Bushmen's minds more deeply. He was less the outsider and idyll-creator than Flaherty had been. One of its greatest virtues was that *The Hunters* was modern. By the 1950s the earlier films had become dated. They were valued and enjoyed, but not unlike the way in which Chaplin's films are enjoyed. *The Hunters* was proof that fine ethnographic films could still be made.

DEAD BIRDS

After working with John Marshall on *The Hunters*, Robert Gardner began making plans for another large expedition. In 1961, he led the Harvard Peabody Expedition to study the Dani, in what was then Netherlands New Guinea (now the Indonesian province of Irian Jaya). Although the Dani had been first reported in 1938 by an expedition from the American Museum of Natural History and were not "unknown" or "untouched" when the Harvard expedition arrived, many Dani were still using stone axes and carrying on warfare with bows and arrows and spears. It was one of the rare chances for anthropologists to observe firsthand these sorts of activities. The standard pattern for ethnography has been for a single ethnographer to work alone and report a single point of view; or, if two ethnographers work together, the results are reported in joint publications as consensus conclusions (e.g., if Bateson and Mead differed in their conclusions about Bali, we have no hint of it). The Harvard Peabody Expedition is practically unique in that it resulted in a number of books, articles, and films by different people (including myself) with different views of the same Dani doing the same things.

Gardner's film *Dead Birds* was shot during the first five months of the expedition. Gardner worked closely with Jan Broekhuijse, a Dutch government anthropologist who had studied the Dani; he also used input from the rest of the expedition; and, of course, he is a trained anthropologist himself. In the summmer of 1962, midway through the editing of *Dead Birds*, he made a return visit to New Guinea and discussed the film with me; and at the end of 1963, after I had been with the Dani for eighteen months, I returned to Cambridge to help with the final editing of the film.

Dead Birds is, like *The Hunters*, still very much in the Flaherty tradition. It is a long inclusive film following Weyak the warrior and Pua the little swineherd as the society moves through a series of war crises. The major events are not reconstructed or staged. Battles and funerals were going on during the filming and are shown in the film as they happened. (The persistent rumors that the Harvard Peabody Expedition instigated or encouraged warfare are untrue. We did, of course, observe warfare, and we did not attempt to discourage it.) Gardner's interpretation of the meaning of war to the Dani or his attributions of thoughts to specific people at specific times can be challenged. For example, I doubt that the Dani are as explicitly philosophical about death as Gardner states (see K. G. Heider 1970:138–140). But our disagreements fall well within the range of acceptable variation in ethnographic interpretation.

Inevitably the film is incomplete as a definitive description of Dani warfare. For example, it was made at the beginning of a long ethnographic study, and not until my third trip to the Dani, in 1968, did I learn the details of another phase of Dani warfare, quite different from the ritual phase shown in *Dead Birds* (see K. G. Heider 1970, 1972b).

But if *Dead Birds* is Flaherty-like in some aspects, Gardner's concept of film tied to ethnographic research owes much to Bateson and Mead. This was not a "film expedition"; it was an ethnographic expedition which coordinated the efforts of three ethnographers (Broekuijse, Gardner, and Heider), a natural historian (Peter Matthiessen), a botanist (Chris Versteegh), a professional still photographer (Eliot Elisofon), and others (Michael Rockefeller and Samuel Putnam); as well as, in the 1968 and 1970 follow-ups, a psychologist (Eleanor Rosch).

Dead Birds is only one of the Harvard Peabody Expedition reports on the Dani. It is also tied into the written ethnographic reports through a lengthy ethnographic companion, or study guide. This describes the ethnography of the Dani vis-à-vis the film and includes Gardner's statement about the making of the film, together with a shot-by-shot analysis of the film keyed to the narration (K. G. Heider 1972b). Thus, *Dead Birds* is not only a dramatic eighty-three-minute account of the Dani, but it is also usable as a thoroughly documented study film.

Dead Birds was in many ways a watershed for ethnographic film. It was made without synchronous sound. In 1960, when the equipment for the expedition was being bought, synchronous sound in New Guinea was still a fantasy; by the mid-sixties, reliable portable synchronous sound equipment was available. Before *Dead Birds*, there was a mere handful of films which could be called ethnography; in the decade since *Dead Birds*, literally dozens have been made.

As *Dead Birds* was being finished, Gardner moved the Film Study Center from the Peabody Museum to Harvard's new Visual Arts Center, where he had at last a major training and production laboratory. During the next years he assisted many people in shooting or editing ethnographic films, and he taught courses in ethnographic films. But, unfortunately, the promise of real cooperation between the Film Study Center and Harvard's anthropology department never developed, and a great opportunity to develop the concepts and practice of ethnographic film was lost.

In the late 1960s, Gardner organized a new ethnographic film project on nomads. After continual frustration in finding a suitable location, he filmed the Afar and Hamar of Ethiopia. The first of these films, *Rivers of Sand*, was released in 1974. Meanwhile, when in Ethiopia, he learned of a group of Nuer in Ethiopia and persuaded Hilary Harris to make a film of them.

THE NUER

The Nuer is a film of images of the incredibly tall thin Nuer and their cattle. Through Evans-Pritchard's ethnographic writings, the Nuer have become one of the "standard," best-known cultures in anthropological literature. Hilary Harris is a professional filmmaker who has been especially interested in filming modern dance and ballet. This shows plainly in *The Nuer*. The film could be titled "The Dance of the Cattle." It is one of the most visually beautiful films ever made, and it shows the rhythm and pace of Nuer life, which no ethnographer could ever capture in words (although it is instructive to compare the film with chapter one, "Interest in Cattle," of Evans-Pritchard's 1940 book). But the film is almost without ethnographic integrity. By this I mean that its principles are cinema aesthetic: its framing, cutting, and juxtaposition of images are done without regard for any ethnographic reality (this point is developed further on p. 79).

There is one hint of progress. While Harris and his assistant, George Breidenbach, were on location, Gardner visited them and shot some scenes in synchronous sound. In the finished film we see an old man evidently responding to questions, describing in the Nuer language what is important to him, especially his cattle. Gardner has been criticized for the *Dead Birds* narration, in which he says what the Dani characters are thinking. Although the thoughts seemed reasonable to me, it is obvious that they strike United States audiences as poetic fiction. Now, with synchronous sound, Gardner is able to let the Nuer speak for themselves (always presuming that the audience will accept the validity of the English translation which follows).

But even if *The Nuer* is ethnographically unsound, it has real use in teaching anthropology. It can give students a general holistic feeling for the people, their cattle, and their environment, helping them to build a kind of cognitive landscape into which they can place Evans-Pritchard's written descriptions of Nuer social organization and ritual.

RIVERS OF SAND

Robert Gardner's first Ethiopian film, *Rivers of Sand* (1974), is about the Hamar people. In this film, Gardner takes the synchronous sound interview technique a step beyond *The Nuer* and builds the entire film around a Hamar woman who sits relaxed before the camera and speaks at great length about her life. She is particularly introspective about her own culture, and so she makes an ideal interpreter for us. Between shots of the woman talking,

Gardner uses sequences of Hamar life which more or less directly illustrate what she has said.

A second important feature of *Rivers of Sand* is the ambitiousness of its subject matter. It attempts to describe the women's role in Hamar society. This seems like a particularly nonvisual subject. It is a matter of moods and attitudes and cultural norms, and not nearly as directly behavioral as house-building or farming or warfare. Yet, Gardner takes on the challenge, criss-crossing back and forth over the subject, building up a sense of it through the visual images and through his narration and through the Hamar woman's words. It is a film without a plot line, and so it often is repetitious. It some-times takes symbolic leaps, as when the images cut from a girl's neck iron to the branding of a cow's neck. And it retains the ambiguity of reality, as when we are told of the pain of whipping, but then see a girl smile as she undergoes it. It is not an easy film to watch or to understand. But Gardner has attempted to move ethnographic film closer to the real concerns of anthropology. That is, more anthropologists are concerned with describing cultural attitudes and values than are trying to describe warfare or house-building.

THE NEW BUSHMAN FILMS

After their collaboration on *The Hunters*, Marshall and Gardner had gone their separate ways. Marshall himself was no longer primarily concerned with the Bushmen. He shot *Titicut Follies* (1968), a powerful view of the Bridgewater Asylum for the Criminally Insane, for Frederick Wiseman. (Wiseman later produced an important series of films on American institu-tions: *High School*, *Basic Training*, *Hospital*, *Law and Order*, and *Juvenile Court*.) Marshall went alone to Pittsburgh, where he made a series of his own police films.

But Marshall's Bushman footage was too important to lie idle. In the mid-1960s, work resumed on Marshall's extensive Bushman footage. Marshall himself was only peripherally involved, since during this time he had turned to filming aspects of U.S. life. Others active in the new Bushman effort were Lorna Marshall, Frank Galvin, a film editor, and Timothy Asch. Asch had studied still photography under Edward Weston and Minor White and had done graduate work in anthropology at Harvard and Boston universities. Asch and the Marshalls set up a large ethnographic film studio in Somerville, Massachusetts (near Cambridge), under the title of Documentary Educa-tional Resources (DER). This became an extraordinarily productive center during the late 1960s and the early 1970s. Here the Asch-Marshall group edited nearly twenty more Bushman films, each a short film on a single subject. The first was *Nlum Tchai* (1966), about the Bushman trance ceremony. The footage, of course, had been shot ten years earlier. And although the ceremony is usually done at night, the Bushmen performed it at dawn when it could be filmed. Wild sound and narration were added.

The editors made an innovative solution to the constant problem of how to make a complex event understandable without resorting to a wordy explanatory narrative. They decided to show the ceremony twice. The first time an explanatory narration was read over still photographs of the action, while the second part of the film just ran the footage of the ceremony with well-synchronized wild sound but without any narration.

Another film in the new Bushman series, *An Argument about a Marriage*, also used this technique. The film shows a complex and heated argument between two groups of Bushmen which had arisen when a woman, who had been deserted by her husband and had married again, was reunited with her first husband and the various people involved tried to sort out their rights and duties. The first part of the film introduces the participants in still photographs, while the narration tries to explain and unravel the argument. The second part of the film retraces the quarrel, with wild sound—actually the dialogue, added later. A few English subtitles are used in the second half of the film to keep the audience up with the argument.

But even with the preliminary explanation and the subtitles, it is almost impossible for most viewers to follow the argument, certainly on the first viewing. The trance ceremony in *Nlum Tchai* is understandable through this approach. But "an argument about marriage" is one of the most difficult subjects for film. Film can easily show how Bushmen argue but not so easily explain the argument itself. Marriage itself is a complex, symbolically charged event; the argument about marriage is an abstract wordy examination of its implications. In order for audiences to really understand *An Argument*, a written companion which can add background details, kinship diagrams, and the like is necessary. In 1974, DER began to distribute study guides for *Nlum Tchai* and their other films (Reichlin 1974a–g; Marshall and Biesele 1974; and Reichlin and Marshall 1974). Previously, printed material had accompanied films only as an occasional extraordinary event, and it was usually only an inadequate page or two. DER took a major step in making the production of an adequate study guide accompaniment a routine part of ethnographic filmmaking.

Like Gardner's *Rivers of Sand*, *An Argument about a Marriage* and some of the other new Bushman films are deliberately pushing the limits of film's ability to deal with complex social behavior. Spearing a seal, hunting a giraffe, or building a house are all much more visual, and thus much more amenable to filmic treatment, than is an argument about a marriage. Most ethnographic films have concentrated on the visual technology. But while the study of material culture (or the material aspects of culture) was a major part of early ethnography, now most ethnologists spend most of their thought on more complex and nonvisual events like arguments about marriages. The Marshall group, and particularly Timothy Asch, are making a rare attempt to use ethnographic film to treat the major concerns of anthropology today.

It is an impressive testimony to the insight and thoroughness of John Marshall's photography that the footage which he shot in the 1950s could be so effectively edited into the films of the 1970s. The next necessary step was taken in 1968, when Asch began a collaboration with Napoleon Chagnon which is a model for ethnographic film. Chagnon had spent nineteen months on an ethnographic study of the Yanomamö, in southern Venezuela. He returned to the United States, wrote up his materials for publication (e.g., 1968), and then, after having digested his understanding of the Yanomamö, returned with Asch to make films. The two were well matched: Asch, the filmmaker with training in anthropology; and Chagnon, the anthropologist who knew the culture and had experience with cinematography (during his earlier trips he had shot very creditable footage on the Yanomamö). And they were able to use synchronous sound equipment. In the summer of 1968, they shot footage for *The Feast*, a thirty-minute film on intervillage feasting, an important feature of Yanomamö life which Chagnon had described and analyzed in chapter four of his Yanomamö monograph (1968:105–117).

The Feast uses the same twofold approach developed for *N/um Tchai* and *An Argument about a Marriage*: an introductory section, with stills in which the narration describes background and events of a particular feast, followed by the running film of the feast with English subtitles which translate statements in the synchronous sound discussion and arguments which take place as the visitors arrive and visitors and hosts discuss gifts and countergifts.

Two years later Asch and Chagnon again collaborated, this time in a much more ambitious project designed to make short films illustrating with the Yanomamö materials the wide range of topics covered in introductory anthropology courses, from subsistence activities to mythology. There were many problems in the collaboration, which Asch has described with unusual frankness (1972). It is a revealing cautionary tale of how even well-conceived ethnographic film projects can be affected by the myriad frustrations of using sophisticated equipment in remote jungles, problems of rapport, and personality differences. In all, they shot some 78,000 feet of film and are in the process of releasing more than forty films. Some of the most important of these, such as *The Ax Fight* and *A Man Called "Bee"*, were released too late to be discussed thoroughly in this book.

The French Movement

During the 1960s, there was a boom in ethnographic film in France under the influence of Jean Rouch, a tremendously active French anthropologist who had been making films in Africa since 1946, and Luc de Heusch, another French anthropologist. Unfortunately there has been little contact and less exchange of ideas between France and North America. The scantiness of the following section only reflects this deplorable situation. But those few French ethnographic films which have reached the United States are vivid testimony to the strength of the French movement, and the publication of Rouch's writings in the United States should go far to correct our ignorance (see Feld 1974; Rouch 1974).

In 1960, Jean Rouch was working with Edgar Morin, a sociologist, on *Chronicle of a Summer* (1961). Using the newest portable 16-mm. cameras and synchronous sound equipment, the filmmakers explored the state of mind of people in Paris in a summer when the Algerian War dominated life. They made no pretense of using omniscient invisible cameras. One or another of the filmmakers often appeared on screen, asking questions or participating in discussions. When the bulk of the film had been edited, the rough cut was screened for the participants. Their reactions to themselves and to the other participants and their evaluations of the truth or falseness of the various scenes were then filmed. This formed the second section of the film. The final section was a sequence which followed Rouch and Morin pacing the halls of the Musée de l'Homme evaluating their own film.

The reality captured by the new synchronous sound, and by the deliberate intrusion of the filmmakers, had a profound effect on French filmmakers like Truffaut and Godard. Rouch is considered a father of French *cinéma vérité*, but he had little effect on ethnographic film. Most ethnographic filmmakers have tried to create the illusion of the ethnographic present, without anthropologist. The possibilities of Rouch's approach are important. It is not just a matter of showing the anthropologist in a scene or two, but of building the films around the inescapable fact that an anthropologist and a filmmaker are on the spot and are interacting with the people and thus influencing behavior.

Likewise, Rouch's technique of showing people reacting to their own images has not yet been followed up in any systematic way. Altogether, by showing behavior, showing how it was filmed, and then chewing over its meaning, *Chronicle of a Summer* achieves a remarkable closure totally lacking in most ethnographic films.

Rouch himself made some dozen other more obviously ethnographic films. Unfortunately, until very recently, these films were not available in the United States, and have had little influence, but they explore in various ways the same approaches used in *Chronicle of a Summer*.

Les Maîtres Fous (1955) focuses on the Haouka, a possession ritual carried out by workers who had come from Mali to Accra, then the capital of the British colony of the Gold Coast. The film opens with shots of the workers in the streets of Accra. Then it follows them through the possession ceremony and finally takes them back again to their labor in Accra, with flashback cuts to remind us visually of the same men who play such different roles, for example, the man who acted the general in the ceremony also acts an army private in Accra. There is a very heavy narration, but it directly complements the visuals. That is, it does not just fill in vaguely relevant or background information, but it explains the wild behavior of the ceremony and also gives an interpretation of the ceremony as a reenactment of the attitudes and rituals of the British colonial officers. Finally, the conclusion suggests that the ritual has a cathartic effect, allowing the natives to mock the British on Sunday in order that they can sanely submit to colonial servitude during the week.

Les Maîtres Fous is a powerful and controversial film; perhaps its power and its controversy stem from similar features. More than most ethnographic films, its visuals and its sounds focus, rather than dissipate, the viewers' attention. The Haouka performers are a disturbing sight: men in trance, seemingly out of control, frothing at the mouth and drinking dog's blood. The film does not try to gloss over or pretty-up that image. It forces the viewer to observe reality, and then leads the viewer into deeper understanding. The film is at the opposite extreme from the banality of the travelogue, which shows all men, however exotic, the same. *Les Maîtres Fous* says that these men are very different from us, and we must understand why. One of Jean Rouch's favorite admonitions to ethnographic filmmakers is "Tell a Story!" But in *Chronicle of a Summer* and *Les Maîtres Fous* (as well as other films like *The Lion Hunters*), he has done much more than that. He has used film to analyze a situation. That is ethnography.

University of California American Indian Series

Most ethnographic filmmaking involves some influence of behavior by filmmakers in the interest of the ethnographic present. For instance, we decided during the filming of *Dead Birds* not to give the Dani red cloth or steel axes as trade goods, and Gardner deliberately avoided showing members of the expedition in the film.

But on occasion, filmmakers have done wholesale re-creation of events. In the 1920s, both Flaherty and the ethnographic fiction films did this. In the 1950s, Samuel A. Barrett, an anthropologist with the Department of Anthropology at the University of California, Berkeley, made a series of films on California Indians (Barrett 1961). They were asked to reenact such old traits as leaching acorns or making a sinew-backed bow. As it happens, some of the most important footage was shot as a spin-off of this project—a two-night curing ceremony performed by a Pomo shaman, Essie Parrish. Two films of the second night have been released (*Sucking Doctor* and its short version, *Pomo Shaman*), but funds ran out before footage of the first night could be edited.

The Netsilik Eskimo Project

The most ambitious film reconstruction project ever mounted was focused on the Netsilik Eskimos of Pelly Bay, Canada. When the Soviets launched their Sputnik in 1958, the United States was shocked into awareness that we were lagging behind in the hard sciences. Government funds were poured into a crash program designed to improve the teaching of science at all levels. But within a few years, social scientists began to be concerned that their fields were being neglected. One result was the establishment of Education Services, Inc. (ESI)—which later became Educational Development Center—in Cambridge, drawing on Harvard and M.I.T. intellectual resources and funded by the National Science Foundation. It was decided that the social sciences could best be represented in the primary grades by anthropology, using the exoticism of other cultures to convey basic concepts. A number of curriculum units were planned, all using carefully designed films. During the early 1960s, ESI contracted for numerous film projects in Iraq, Mexico, New Guinea, Kenya, and Canada.

The only unit which was successfully completed was the one on the Netsilik Eskimos, emphasizing ecological adaptation to an extreme environment. The Netsilik series was produced by Quentin Brown, and two anthropologists, Asen Balikci and Guy Marie de Roussellet, worked closely with the camera crews in the field. An ethnographic present of 1919 was used. The Netsilik who worked on the project re-created the clothing and houses and subsistence activities in use forty years earlier, drawing on their own memories and the report of the anthropologist Knud Rasmussen, who had visited the area in 1923 (Balikci and Brown 1966). Nine thirty-minute films were produced. Each was a long, thorough view of a set of activities associated with a particular season, such as a fishing weir or hunting caribou. The films have excellently dubbed natural sound but no narration or even subtitles. They are designed as part of an inclusive educational package and are accompanied by teachers' manuals, student exercise books, and the like. The films are intentionally close to raw data, and students are supposed to raise questions and, with their teachers' help, reach some conclusions. They use Flaherty's technique of visual suspense very effectively. For example, in *Winter Sea-Ice Camp*, part one, a man performs a mysterious operation, icing a hair on to a bone and laying it over a hole in the ice. Only slowly does the viewer realize that this will move when the seal comes for air, signaling the hunter to thrust his spear into the hole. Because of their pedagogical purpose, the Netsilik films focus on technology almost to the exclusion of social life, and there is no hint of Eskimo religious practices. The Netsilik had long since been Christianized, and perhaps they were unwilling or unable to reenact their pagan practices.

Australia

The longest tradition of ethnographic film exists in Australia, where Spencer first shot aboriginal dancers with a crude camera in 1904. Mountford in the 1940s and Ian Dunlop and Roger Sandall in the 1960s have continued to record aboriginal rituals and subsistence activities, but there has been little advance in the ethnographicness of the films. When anthropologists were involved, they were used as sound men and assistants, not researchers. Recently there has been a growing concern among aboriginal men to preserve and protect the sanctity and secrecy of their own ceremonies. This has meant a virtual halt in the publication of descriptions and analyses of ceremonies in forms which might become available to aboriginal women and uninitiated men. Now many films on rituals cannot be shown in Australia at all.

The Natives' View

When they offer interpretations of behavior, ethnographic films have generally been negligent in disentangling native from anthropological levels of interpretation. In ethnology, the distinction is essential. Two recent projects have attempted to capture the native view on film, but they have taken very different approaches.

THE NAVAJO FILM THEMSELVES

Sol Worth, a professor of communications, and John Adair, an anthropologist, with the assistance of Richard Chalfen, then a graduate student working with Worth, conducted an experiment in 1966 in which Navajo Indians made films about their own culture.

On the (Whorf-Sapir) assumption that the structure of language in some sense reflects or shapes the world view of speakers of that language, and on the assumption that film, as a form of expression, is in some way analogous to language, Worth and Adair hypothesized that films made by Navajos would be in some fundamental sense Navajo.

Some twenty films were made by eight Navajos, and ten of these are in distribution. None of the Navajos had used a movie camera before, and it is not clear how much of the results to attribute to inexperience and how much to "Navajo-ness." Most of the filmmakers had seen Hollywood films and television, and one was a self-professed admirer of French cinema, but one can only guess at the implications of these various influences.

And apparently no one fluent in Navajo had analyzed the data. Worth and Adair do make a convincing case for two major Navajo influences. First, most of the films have long sequences of someone walking. In the *Navajo Silversmith*, fifteen minutes are spent on showing the silversmith walking in search of materials, and only five minutes on actually casting and finishing silver. This walking theme is very prominent in Navajo myths.

Also, the general Navajo avoidance of direct eye contact is reflected in the general absence of full-face close-ups in the Navajo films. But of course, to a non-Navajo these features would only be puzzling, or not even noticed, without Worth and Adair's analysis. Ethnography has traditionally involved translation, explanation, and analysis of one culture into the idiom of another. If Worth and Adair are right, then Navajo films would be somehow "in Navajo" and would therefore be the raw material for ethnography, not ethnography itself. The most valuable aspect of the project was to raise the question of the culturally specific nature of films. The implications of this are of great importance to ethnographic films. There is a great need for more research in this direction.

JAPANESE TEA

The Worth and Adair approach was to give Navajos film equipment but minimal instruction or direction, to encourage them to make films, and then to see if the resulting films contained anything which seemed specifically Navajo.

Donald Rundstrom and Ronald Rundstrom, with the help of Clinton Bergum, took a very different approach in *The Path*, a film of the Japanese tea ceremony. After long and intensive study of the tea ceremony and its philosophy, they designed the film not just to depict it but also to embody the aesthetic principles in its shots and sequences. They made a studied attempt to show the tea ceremony not only in the visual depiction but also in the very structure of the film. The Rundstroms were particularly concerned to show the yin-yang balancing of opposites and the management of energy, or the energy flow. The film is a mixture of ethnographic explanation and nearly inaccessible raw materials. It does show the progress of a tea ceremony as two women walk through a formal garden into a tea house, where their hostess serves them tea. The occasional narrative gives words of explanation, instruction, or Zen obfuscation from famous tea masters. On the other hand, the filmmakers did not attempt to have the narration point out the subtler, deeper structural motifs. They have solved this problem by preparing an ethnographic companion for the film which describes in detail the history of the Japanese tea ceremony and the aesthetic principles of *do*, the way, and recounts the making of the film (Rundstrom, Rundstrom, and Bergum 1973).

Institutionalization in the United States

During the decade since 1963, the year in which *Dead Birds* appeared, ethnographic film shared in the rich growth of the social sciences and became institutionalized, bureaucratized, and established. In the spring of 1964, there had been a conference at the University of California, Berkeley, on filmmaking in anthropology. But as late as 1965, there were virtually no programs, publications, or regular meetings on ethnographic film. In the next years, much happened. The Program in Ethnographic Film (PIEF) was established, slowly grew, and by 1973, under the leadership of Jay Ruby, had become the Society for the Anthropology of Visual Communication (SAVICOM), an incorporated organization under the wing of the American Anthropological Association (AAA); a film catalogue, Films for Anthropological Teaching, which was begun in 1966 with listings of less than one hundred films and was distributed out of Robert Gardner's office at Harvard, had, by 1972, appeared in a fifth edition with nearly five hundred films and was being distributed by the American Anthropological Association in Washington, D.C. The *PIEF Newsletter*, begun by Jay Ruby and Carroll Williams in 1969, continued as the newsletter for SAVICOM and was then incorporated in the *Anthropology Newsletter* of the AAA. Since 1972, another newsletter, *Media Anthropologist*, edited by C. A. Jones, has been published from Prince George Community College; and, in 1974, SAVICOM began a more formal publication series under the editorship of Sol Worth. Since 1966, ethnographic film sessions have been a regular feature of the AAA annual meetings, and in 1969, Jay Ruby began the annual Conference on Visual Anthropology at Temple University in Philadelphia. There have been formal programs in ethnographic film at UCLA, Temple, the Chicago campus of the University of Illinois, and California State University at San Francisco; and, in the summer of 1972, the Summer Institute in Visual Anthropology was held in Santa Fe, New Mexico. The National Anthropological Film Center has been established in the Smithsonian Institution under the directorship of E. Richard Sorenson; and since 1965, ethnographic films have been reviewed in the *American Anthropologist*, first under the editorship of Gordon Gibson, and then of Timothy Asch.

Along with this remarkable flurry of activity, and presumably stimulated in good part by it, has been a tremendous increase in the pace of ethnographic filmmaking, much of it having a more ethnographic approach.

Chapter 3

The Attributes of Ethnographic Film

In the first chapter we discussed the general nature of film and of ethnography and what we can expect of the two together; the second chapter was a selective foray into the history of ethnographic film designed to trace the development of various ideas which could make film more ethnographic. In this chapter we shall analyze in greater detail those various attributes of film which affect its ethnographicness. This will be a critical examination and a guide to understanding and judging ethnographic films of the past, and it will suggest standards for making ethnographic films in the future. It is an attempt to systematize what has emerged after fifty years of ethnographic filmmaking. Of course, there are those for whom films are purely art, to be experienced and appreciated in darkened rooms, and there are filmmakers for whom making films is an intuitive, aesthetic, emotional act of creation. For them this book is bound to appear as the overintellectualization of an essentially experiential enterprise. But it is basic to ethnography, as well as the other social sciences, that we have a rational explicit methodology. And thus films which attempt to achieve ethnographicness must share this quality of rational, explicit, methodology.

The discussion in this chapter is ordered around several attributes which are common to all films, however ethnographic they may be. But each attribute has some value or values which are more ethnographic than another value or values. Each one is a criterion for judging the ethnographicness of a film. Taken together, the attributes allow one to make a profile description of a film, and they provide a basis for saying in what respects some films are more ethnographic than others. I still resist any attempt to define ethnographic film, or to say whether a particular film is or is not ethnographic. But the use of the attribute profile will make quite explicit what is meant by ethnographicness in film and will allow us to judge on the basis of a complex but explicit set of criteria the extent to which a film is ethnographic.

This chapter is divided into three parts, each a more systemic treatment of the attributes than the preceding part. First we shall explore at some length the principles underlying each attribute. Then we shall make a succinct definition of each attribute and diagram that attribute as an attribute dimension with examples of specific films which illustrate the various points along this dimension; and in the final part we shall present the attributes as a grid on which a profile of ethnographicness can be drawn for any particular film.

The Attributes

BASIC TECHNICAL COMPETENCE

One of the most unambiguous criteria for any film is simple technical cinematographic competence: the images should be focused and exposed so as to be visible; the sound, especially when it is in the language of the intended audience, should be clear enough to be audible; and the editing should be free of accidental mistakes and errors due to incompetence.

Under normal circumstances the most egregious errors are avoided. But ethnographic films are usually shot and recorded in remote locations, often of unique events, and frequently by minimally trained people. Since ethnographic filmmakers usually do not see their footage until they have returned from the field, there is often no opportunity to reshoot any botched scenes or to shoot additional fill-in footage which they realize that they need only several months and many thousands of miles too late.

Basic technical competence is remarked on only when it is absent. I doubt that anyone will ever review an ethnographic film with the words, "it was in focus throughout." On the other hand, filmmakers often condemn an ethnographic film on the grounds of technical errors, saying that it contains more such mistakes than would be tolerated in a "professional" film.

If we think in terms of ethnographic film, however, we must consider the extent to which technical errors hinder the ethnographic effectiveness of a film. It is possible that a film could be so out of focus throughout that an audience simply couldn't understand the images or that a narration could be so badly recorded that it was inaudible. In such extreme cases it is unlikely that the film would be distributed. But let us consider some less blatant errors.

Focus. Appeals to Santiago, about a Chiapas (Mexico) Mayan ceremony, has scenes which were shot in very soft focus. The film is quite usable. Indeed, nonfilmmakers often overlook the lack of sharpness. However, once audiences are made aware of it, the focus becomes more and more distracting throughout the film. The effectiveness of the film seems to be directly related to how focus-conscious the audience is.

In editing *Dani Sweet Potatoes*, I faced a common problem: one shot of a technological sequence was noticeably out of focus. Ethnographically, that shot was necessary to establish the continuity of building a steam bundle for cooking sweet potatoes; cinematographically, the shot was poor quality but was just adequate to show that step in the process. I had three choices: I could have discarded the total film, edited it with an information gap, or edited it with a technological lapse. It was not a happy choice, but ethnographic considerations overrode cinematographic considerations and I chose the third alternative.

Exposure. Proper exposure poses even more hazards for the ethnographic filmmaker than does proper focus. Electronic exposure meters may break down in extreme temperature and humidity conditions; worse, they may just malfunction slightly; film stored in tropical heat may suffer color deterioration, especially after it has been exposed; much important behavior takes place under poorly lighted conditions indoors, at night, or both.

Very poorly printed copies of films can come from commercial laboratories, and, unfortunately, when universities buy prints they usually have no way of judging whether the prints are of reasonable quality. I have seen two or three prints of *Dead Birds* whose color was so washed out that they certainly should have never left the lab. But they were paid for in good faith by universities (in one case by a museum). And the color quality of the dyes in even the best print is likely to deteriorate after it has been through fifty or one hundred screenings and has been stored under conditions where neither temperature nor humidity is rigorously controlled.

Probably ethnographic films never are released with shots whose exposure is so poor that the images are actually unreadable. But, like poor focus, marginal exposure can be distracting to an audience. I have the feeling, however, that although exposure problems may be more noticeable than focus problems, they are more acceptable and so actually less distracting.

Sound. Problems with sound are often created or compounded in the projection process. Faulty threading of a projector or inadequate speakers may render even quite good sound inaudible.

Sound quality is particularly critical for a narration which is in English and is meant to be understood. Since the usual narration is recorded toward the end of the editing process, it is normally of quite satisfactory quality. If mistakes are made, they can easily be rerecorded. But if the narration is made from field recordings, irremediable faults may be included. Then difficult choices, similar to those involving footage, arise: whether or not to use sound which is technically wanting but which would contribute ethnographicness to the film. This problem is heightened in films which use statements made in English by people for whom English is a second language, and so speak it with heavy accents. *Floating in the Air*, about Tamils in Malaysia, and *The Turtle People*, about Miskito Indians in Nicaragua, are examples of this. In both films, the statements by the people in English add much to the sense of reality, but for most viewers the English is simply not understandable. *Forty Seven Cents*, about an American Indian reservation, solves this problem well by the very obvious device of English subtitles clarifying obscure English.

Jump cuts. Another kind of error in ethnographic films is film breaks, or jump cuts, where a central section of a shot is lost and the two ends are spliced together, giving the effect of an awkward jump in the action. It is often difficult to account for jump cuts. They may be errors in the original footage caused by stopping the camera for a quick rewind, or accidents in cutting, intentionally retained by the filmmaker; or they may be breaks caused in screening the films. Too many film distributors will continue to rent a print long after it has accumulated numerous repair splices.

Some cinematographers usually try to avoid jump cuts. One standard alternative is to insert a cut-away shot; but, as we will discuss later, this is usually a shot taken out of context, and so it often impairs the ethnographic integrity of the film. Another solution is to use a dissolve (where one scene dissolves into the next) to bridge the gap. Not only does the dissolve eliminate the necessity for irrelevant footage, but it also indicates the passage of time which in fact has occurred in a jump cut.

All these errors are unintentional in the sense that they are not desired effects. They have been retained in ethnographic films either through ignorance (usually because they were simply not noticed in editing) or because of an ethnographic judgment that the content of a particular shot was more important than achieving a more cinematographically competent film.

DISTORTIONS

It is inconceivable that an ethnographic film could be made in such a way that it did not distort or alter or select its images of reality in a myriad of ways. Therefore it gets us nowhere to ask if a film is subjective, or if it distorts reality. The answer to both questions has to be yes.

And, as we discussed in chapter one, ethnographies also distort reality in many ways. One could make a very strong argument to the effect that, since both films and ethnographies do distort reality, there is no point in discussing reality or truth at all. This argument may have a beneficial effect in freeing cinema-as-art from false constraints. But here we are talking about cinema in the service of science. Social scientists (and even physical scientists) are well aware of the distortions and the subjectivity and the selections which enter their research. But at the same time, the scientific goals are phrased in terms of truth, or at the very least, truths; and scientists speak without embarrassment of the possibility of being more or less accurate. Because of this, the nature of a review of a monograph in *Science* is very different from that of a film review in *Film Quarterly*.

This book is to some extent a treatise on the curious relationship of the scientist to truth. As we explored the implications of ethnographic film in chapter one, we began to look at truth and distortion in an unusual light.

Now I will reformulate the position of this book. I start with the assumption that the task of ethnography is to achieve a truthful and realistic description and analysis of cultural and social behavior, and I assume that this task is within the reach of a normal ethnographer. It follows that ethnographers attempt to achieve this in their work and that critics base their judgments on the notion that truth and reality are achievable. Although there are many different sorts of ethnographic approaches, each has its own criteria for truth and realism, and, therefore, each can be carried out more or less adequately. (The question of which approach is best for any or all situations is a central issue in anthropology, but we can quite comfortably bypass it here.)

In other words, ethnography gives us many ways to get at truths and realities. But the acceptance of many ways and many truths and many realities does not mean that everything is equally true. It means that for each of the ways there are truths and nontruths, realities and unrealities. This is basically a position of broad-minded dogmatism.

In the following sections we will discuss the various sorts of distortions which are found in ethnographic filmmaking, and we will try to evaluate the degree to which these distortions threaten the integrity of an ethnographic film. I have chosen the word "distortion" with due thought and some trepidation. Obviously, the word is not used in a totally negative sense. It is meant to denote all the alterations in the representations of reality which take place during the translation of behavior from original occurrence to the final image on the movie screen.

There are two main sorts of distortions: the one occurs when the filmmakers, intentionally or inadvertently, cause alterations in the behavior which they are filming; and the other occurs during the filmmaking process itself, through the selective acts of shooting or of editing.

Direct Distortions of Behavior

1. *Inadvertent distortion. The effect of intrusion and camera conscious-*

ness. Most ethnographic films purport to show naturally occurring behavior. All ethnographic films have used cameras which are visible and thus intrusive into the behavioral space of the people being filmed. No ethnographic films have been made of people for whom camera and film crew are a natural part of their behavioral space.

There is the paradox.

In any ordinary ethnographic research the ethnographer can only guess at the effect which his presence has on the behavior which he is observing. He can never observe it in his own absence. In ethnographic film this bind is writ large because the camera is often wielded by a stranger, perhaps assisted by a film crew, and so is far more obtrusive than a single ethnographer poking about, notebook in hand, making observations and interviewing people. Few ethnographers have ever tried to answer the question of the effect of their own presence. It is one of the conventions of anthropology that we usually ignore it.

In fact, few ethnographers do much more than the obligatory acknowledgment that they were there. In his famous introduction to *Argonauts of the Western Pacific* in 1922, Bronislaw Malinowski insisted that ethnographers must explain how they gathered their data. This seems like a minimal demand, but forty-five years later, David Maybury-Lewis, in the introduction to his *Akwe-Shavante Society*, could still regret that "anthropologists are frequently reticent about the circumstances of their field work" (1967:xix).

Actually, while the manner of obtaining data is relatively easy to describe, the extent to which the data reflect the intrusion of the ethnographer is much harder to determine. Ethnographers can write around their presence, creating a conventionally fictionalized account of events which might be called "the ethnographic absence." (A permutation of the phrase "the ethnographic present," referring to another convention of ethnography, in which we describe cultures not as they are but as they presumably existed in some untouched primal state.) But even though the ethnographer can write in the mode of the "ethnographic absence," an ethnographic filmmaker usually cannot, since the camera uncompromisingly records the effects of the intrusion and film audiences can easily sense mugging and other forms of camera consciousness.

How does filming affect behavior? Only a few anthropologists have even considered the problem in print. Margaret Mead, writing about the study which she and Gregory Bateson carried out in Bali in 1936–1938 and which involved extensive still and movie photography, suggests that the presence of the cameras had little effect on the Balinese: "They were unself-conscious about photography, accepting it as a part of a life which was in many ways always lived on a stage" (1970:259). Bateson, writing specifically about the still photography (in Bateson and Mead 1942:49), discussed the factors "which contributed to diminish camera consciousness in our subjects." But these are denials of influence and not real considerations of the extent of the influence. And in fact, in many scenes in the Bateson and Mead Balinese films, especially those which show casual family interaction in a courtyard, the adults do seem to be acting in reference to Bateson and Mead and even appear to be asking them for instructions.

Adam Kendon and Andrew Ferber came to similar conclusions in their study of greeting behavior, where they had set up three 16-mm. movie cameras at an outdoor birthday party near New York City. On the basis of the participants' reports and their own observations, they felt that the people were "almost completely unaffected by the cameras" (1973:598).

But the opposite opinion is stated by Edmund Carpenter. He describes an experiment with natives of the Sepik River area in New Guinea. He first used a hidden camera to film people who were unaware that they were even being observed; then he made them camera-conscious and filmed them in that state. Carpenter claims that the presence of the camera totally altered their behavior: "Almost invariably, body movements became faster, jerky, without poise or confidence. Faces that had been relaxed froze or alternated between twitching & rigidity" (1972:138).

Unfortunately, Carpenter so far has published only the most anecdotal accounts of this experiment, and since his footage is not generally available, his findings are difficult to evaluate. But his challenge to ethnographic film cannot easily be brushed aside. He has raised a crucial question which should be subjected to rigorous investigation.

Anthropologists who use film to record and analyze body movement, or nonverbal behavior, often support the position that cameras have no significant effect on behavior with an interesting argument. They claim that they are looking at patterns of behavior which have been so thoroughly learned and are so unconscious that they will not be easily altered, or, if they are altered, the alteration is only on a surface level and does not affect the basic cultural movements.

But these arguments would concern only the most overlearned and unconscious aspects of behavior. To draw an analogy to language is appropriate here. It is one thing to suggest that a person who knows that his speech is being recorded will not make significant changes in his vocabulary, pronunciation, or grammar, but quite another thing to say that the content of his speech is unchanged. And in the behavior which is recorded in ethnographic film, what is being done is quite as important as how it is being done.

Pat Loud (the mother and wife in the television series "An American Family") described vividly how her family altered its behavior at the first suggestion that they would be filmed:

> Immediately the Heisenberg Principle—anything observable is changed by the fact of being observed—went into effect and we all became charming, amusing, photogenic, and generally irresistible. We did our number . . . it might not be apparent . . . , but we always put on a good front. . . . We were quite capable of keeping up a running ho-ho banter which perfectly achieved its aim of hiding anything either of us felt about anything. (Loud and Johnson 1974:89)

> You can't forget the camera, and everybody's instinct is to try and look as good as possible for it, all the time, and to keep kind of snapping along being active, eager, cheery, and productive. Out go those moments when you're just in a kind of nothing period, hibernating until you move onto the next thing. (Loud and Johnson 1974:102)

It is interesting to compare Pat Loud's "native" account with that of Alan and Susan Raymond, who shot most of the film for "An American Family" (1973). The Raymonds make no attempt to evaluate the effect of their presence on the Loud family and indeed show no awareness at all that they had any effect. How can we judge these contradictory claims? We have no comparable "native" statements for any other ethnographic film. In the case of "An American Family" it is clear that at least one subject felt that the film account of her life was wildly inaccurate, while the filmmakers felt that it was accurate. There are obvious possibilities for bias in both accounts. We can take the easiest (but long-delayed) first step and raise the question of the effect of camera intrusion on behavior. The next step, answering this question, is much harder, but should be attempted.

Incidentally, camera consciousness may be as hard to simulate as it is to avoid. In Alfred Hitchcock's *Rebecca*, there are scenes of home movies which Laurence Olivier and Joan Fontaine took of each other on their honeymoon. In the film as a whole, both Olivier and Fontaine give outstandingly convincing performances, but, in this film-within-a-film sequence, neither can capture the easily recognizable symptoms of camera consciousness. They are simply too much in control of themselves.

Relative energy level. A major determinant of disruption is the relative energy level of the event being filmed and the filmmakers. In the Haouka ceremony possession scenes of *Les Maîtres Fous*, or in the funeral and battle scenes of *Dead Birds*, the activity itself had such high energy that it absorbed all the attention of the people and the cameras were ignored. Kendon and Ferber are quite explicit about this factor in their discussion of camera consciousness at the birthday party, where they claim that "the event gathered its own momentum and proved to be absorbing enough for both adults and children for them not to care very much about the filming" (1973:598).

But typically in shots of casual activities, where not much is happening and the energy level is comparatively low, attention is drawn to the camera. Then the camera crew becomes a significant part of the total behavior. This is especially evident in *The Village*, where Mark McCarty tried to capture the subtle ambiance of rural Irish life. But McCarty's own ebullience behind the camera completely overbalanced the low energy level of the behavior he was filming.

In its most blatant form, camera consciousness is marked by people making eye contact with the camera. But there is a subtler form, marked by body stiffness and "unnatural" movement, which audiences can sense even when they cannot precisely describe the cues which they have used.

Mugging. A more extreme sign of intrusion is mugging, a stylized performance in which people interact in exaggerated manner with the camera, making silly faces and gestures. Every photographer has had experiences with subjects mugging in this way. It is a sign of extreme unease at being confronted, not with a familiar human face, but with a glass and metal contraption. Mugging may be a kind of exaggeration of gesture into which a person intuitively feels pushed in order to communicate through the opaque barrier of the camera machinery. As shouting is an exaggerated voice level necessary to span physical distance, so mugging is exaggerated nonverbal communication necessary to span the machine-created distance.

Photographic sophistication. In a few cases, camera consciousness has been minimal simply because the people do not know what a camera is. These naïve situations are rare and will soon be nonexistent except for very young children. In 1961, when *Dead Birds* was being filmed in West New Guinea, the Dani had had no experience with cameras, and we did not explain what cameras were, since we felt that there was a danger that they would misunderstand and feel threatened. Later, as I came to know the Dani better I realized that this was an unnecessary fear. But in 1968, when I visited the Dani, I left a Polaroid camera with a missionary, who proceeded to use it quite openly. As a result, by 1970 most Dani in that area were extremely camera conscious and mugged at the sight of a camera. Despite this, a Japanese-Indonesian television crew which filmed the major Pig

Feast in 1970 (see K. G. Heider 1972b) found what we had experienced nine years earlier: when important ceremonies were going on, the Dani completely ignored the cameras.

2. *Intentional distortion of behavior. Alteration of material culture.* Nanook's igloo is the classic case of a filmmaker altering material culture. Flaherty found that a normal Eskimo igloo was simply too small and too dark to allow him to shoot inside it. His solution was to have the Eskimo build a half-igloo shell, twice normal size, in which he could show Eskimo home life. This was deliberate distortion done to achieve reality. The film is able to show something of Eskimo life inside the igloo. We see the family undressing, getting under the fur covers, going to sleep and waking. It is hardly a comprehensive treatment, but this is really the only sequence in which the whole family is established as a family unit. The drawback, however, is that we are given a false impression of the size of the igloo living space. And we are given a false sense of the inside temperature when we see Nanook and his family strip off their clothes when it is obviously cold enough for their breath to condense. But Flaherty decided that the advantages of distortion outweighed the disadvantages.

But there is a second decision: should the filmmaker reveal such artifice, and how? On the whole, filmmakers are reluctant to discuss this, except informally. From an ethnographic standpoint, however, we must know in considerable detail what distortion occurred. To a great degree the ethnographic integrity of a film depends on the extent to which we can learn of the distortions. It is certainly difficult both to create artifice and to reveal it in the course of a film. In most cases it is sufficient to describe it elsewhere, in writing. For example, many of Flaherty's distortions are now well-known from the many books and articles written about him and his films. But most other reconstructed films, such as the Netsilik Eskimo series, the American Indian series, and the desert people series, have fallen far short in desirable explanation of how they recreated their behavior and artifacts.

Reality can be deceptive, too. Ronald Rundstrom has described (personal communication) how the carnations in the teahouse in *The Path* were chosen and arranged carefully by the filmmakers and the tea mistress to enhance the autumnal mood of that particular tea ceremony. But somehow, perhaps because of the color balance of the film, or the wide-angle lens, in the finished film the carnations are too obtrusive.

Interruption of behavior. The filmmaker may interrupt behavior, breaking its flow in order that cameras may be moved, so as to get a variety of different angle shots. Then the footage can be edited together to create an even flow. In *Dead Birds*, for example, during a minor curing ceremony a man makes a feathered reed wand and gives it to two boys who run shouting out of the compound. The boys are seen from inside the compound running out, and then in the next shot picked up outside running down the path. Gardner stopped the boys as they got outside, followed and set up his camera outside, and then filmed them as they resumed running. It would be difficult to argue that this made any significant change in the boys' running behavior.

On the other hand, in *The Path* each shot was set up separately for optimal camera angle, rehearsed, and shot. The filmmakers felt that the women had so routinized their movements after years of training that they could resume the flow of action at will. However, they acknowledged that this filming approach eliminated the easy social chatter which accompanies the movements. Knowing this, the viewer can study the film for its description of movement and gesture but is warned not to use it to study the tea ceremony as social interaction.

The use of two cameras can get around this problem. *Tidikawa and Friends*, made by Jeff and Su Doring in New Guinea, is one of the rare ethnographic films which has used two cameras to good effect in the field. One memorable scene of a man felling a large tree cuts from a close-up of the falling tree to a long shot, leaving no doubt that two cameras were covering the same event. The major drawback, of course, is that the effective use of two cameras creates a larger and more intrusive film crew.

"Staged" behavior. Casual critics of ethnographic films often condemn a film on the grounds that some scenes are "staged." By this they seem to imply that the behavior is not accurate because it was directed by the filmmaker. This is in fact a very complex question. To evaluate "staged" behavior we must know the circumstances of filming and the culture being filmed.

There are two related questions: if the events in a film were not purely spontaneous, then what was the role of the filmmaker? And if the events were in some manner instigated or encouraged by the filmmaker, were they events in the current cultural repertory or were they revived after more or less long abeyance?

Although these facts should be part of the public record of any film with scientific pretensions, they can only be established for a few ethnographic films, and then more often from external published account and oral tradition (i.e., rumor or gossip) than from evidence within the film itself.

Wedding of Palo is a good example of such knowledge, because we know that it is a scripted, acted Eskimo love story. But it was directed by Knud Rasmussen, a knowledgeable Arctic anthropologist and traveler who was himself half Eskimo, and it was acted in Greenland by Eskimos. One scene is of a song duel between Palo and Samo, rivals for the love of the girl. The song duel is a classic conflict-resolution institution, well-known from the literature on the Eskimo. On these grounds one can say with fair confidence that the song duel in *Wedding of Palo* is accurate both in its particulars and in its context. But of course that particular song duel never happened. And it is inconceivable that a naturally occurring song duel could have been filmed in anything approaching the detail of that one.

At the other extreme, *The Sky Above and the Mud Below*, a popular travelogue about a trip across New Guinea in 1960, is noteworthy for its obvious manipulations and exaggerated claims. For example, in an early scene the camera is traveling up a river in the Asmat and suddenly meets a huge war party of Asmaters in dozens of canoes bearing down on it. Only the most credulous viewer could believe that it is accidental. Obviously the "war party" was arranged for the film. Illegitimate? Not completely, for these *are* Asmat warriors, paddling in the Asmat manner.

Soon thereafter we witness an Asmat initiation ceremony. But it is one which had not been performed for years and was revived for the benefit of the film crew—apparently the roof of the house was even removed to provide enough light for the filming. However, this ceremony is done by Asmaters and must be to some extent genuine. The trouble is that most viewers cannot separate the genuine from that which was dictated by the French film crew.

The behavior in the Netsilik films is also a puzzle. We know that an ethnographic present of 1919 was recreated in the 1960s. It is easy to see how artifacts can be reconstructed from drawings. But how is a complex process like hunting or fishing or housebuilding reconstructed? How much came from the actors' memories, how much from their parents' memories, and how much from Rasmussen's writings? These are the sorts of things which we need to know. They are described briefly by Balikci and Brown (1966), and we can expect Balikci to spell them out in greater detail in the near future.

Triggering behavior. Another practice which is similar to reconstruction is that of triggering the behavior. This is not a matter of reviving some behavior from the past, but of influencing the timing for some behavior in current usage.

Bateson distinguished between photographs which are posed and those taken when the ethnographer merely triggers the behavior: "In a great many instances, we created the *context* in which the notes and photographs were taken, e.g., by paying for the dance or asking a mother to delay the bathing of her child until the sun was high, but this is very different from posing photographs. Payment for theatrical performances is the economic base upon which the Balinese theater depends, and the extra emphasis given to the baby served to diminish the mother's awareness that she was to be photographed" (Bateson and Mead 1942:50).

With this distinction Bateson was trying to make the point that some distortions are good (or at least acceptable) while others are unacceptable. But the matter is much more complex, and it depends greatly on the sorts of data to which one is referring. In order to evaluate how justifiable it was, we need to know what role the filmmakers played and just how they distorted, or "created the context" of, an event. But even more, we need to have some evaluation by the ethnographer of the result of that distortion. For example, in *Desert People* the opening titles tell us that the film was made of an Australian aborigine family which had been on a mission station for only three months when it agreed to return to the Western Desert to work with the film crew. That is important and necessary information. But there is no hint whether this might have had any effect on the family's behavior. Were they hunting for food, or were they hunting animals for the camera and then having bully beef with the film crew? And if the latter is true, did it make any difference?

In the middle of filming *Dead Birds*, the leaders of one Dani sib said that they would like to perform the *wam kanekhe*, a renewal ceremony for their sacred stones, but unfortunately they did not have enough pigs; however, if we would pay for the necessary pigs, they could perform the ceremony and we could see it. We paid, they performed, and we watched and filmed. I am still not fully certain what was really going on. We did contribute to the ceremony. But were they planning it anyway and saw an opportunity to make us pay for it? Had our expressed interest in seeing their sacred stones planted in their minds the idea of killing two birds with one set of pigs? As the ethnographer, I should know, but I do not. However, I have no reason to suspect that our role in the ceremony significantly altered the performance of the ceremony as seen in the film or on the level I was able to describe it. (If I had reached a deeper command of the Dani language and culture by that point and had been making a careful study of ceremonial exchange, the data would have been anomalous, with pigs coming from the expedition and not from other Dani.)

I feel hesitant about writing about this incident, partly because I cannot give a satisfactory account of all its subtle complexities, and partly because I am sensitive to the persistent rumors that we instigated war among the Dani. We did not, but the rumor is more interesting than the denial and will undoubtedly persist. That is the problem about even describing the situation of this ceremony. It is liable to be misunderstood and turned into a claim that we paid for ceremonies. This is at best a very partial truth, falsified by being stripped of its context. But it must be discussed, for the question of intervention is one which faces many ethnographic filmmakers, and indeed, many ethnographers. It is important to understand and describe these situations.

A similar situation lies behind the scenes of the *gar* initiation ceremony in *The Nuer*, according to Robert Gardner (personal communication). George Breidenbach was alone with the Nuer when an initiation took place but was unable to film it because his camera batteries were not charged. Later, the Nuer told him of two more boys who should have been initiated, but, because of the disruption of a smallpox epidemic, there was not enough beer available to hold a proper ceremony. Breidenbach offered to supply the beer, and the two boys were initiated. Unfortunately, because of his lack of understanding of the ceremony, the scenes are very incomplete. But there is no reason to doubt the integrity of what he did shoot, since it agrees well with Evans-Pritchard's description of the initiation.

Most films which show reconstructed or reenacted behavior simply present it straight as an unacknowledged sort of ethnographic present. Only a very few films indicate in an introductory title or the narration that the behavior is reconstructed. But of course even when this is said, all it does is to serve notice that something is wrong. There is a certain amount of verbal tradition floating around the ethnographic film world—usually misinformed—describing how the scenes were made. It is paradoxical that one can learn more about the technical illusions of feature films, whose purpose is illusion, than about manipulation of reality in ethnographic films, whose purpose is reality.

The Moontrap is a remarkable film because it shows not only the reconstruction event but also the process of that reconstruction. One of the filmmakers, Michael Brault, had worked as cameraman on Jean Rouch's *Chronicle of a Summer*, and *The Moontrap* reflects and extends Rouch's vision of reality in film.

We are told in the opening titles of *The Moontrap* that the National Film Board camera crew encouraged the people of a small French-Canadian community on an island in the St. Lawrence River to revive their custom of trapping beluga whales. The film follows one man as he tries to organize the whale trapping. He discusses it with men who were old enough to have participated in it forty years earlier; he searches the town archives for records of how the task was organized; the matter is discussed at a town meeting; and outlines of the last whale trap are located in the river mud at low tide. The idea of the enterprise begins to have a life of its own.

The great virtue of this approach is that it does much more than show how some people once trapped whales. It does that, of course, but it also shows the meaning of the past for the present.

The Moontrap has the best of two worlds: It does record in detail an interesting and unusual technological process of the past (a film of the same villagers repairing their television sets would not have been as interesting or valuable); and it manages to show how that technological process is embedded in its social context. The film cannot recapture the social context of the original whale trapping, of course, but it does follow out the reverberations of the effort to revive the whale trapping in personal, political, and even religious terms. It was on this score of contextualization that the Netsilik Eskimo films were weakest, for although they also showed old technology, it was re-created for the camera and not placed in the real context of the community. And so despite many nice moments of interpersonal interaction, the Netsilik films are primarily films of individuals-cum-technology, not of technology in context. Of course, the filmmakers of *The Moontrap* were working more or less within their own (French-Canadian) culture, a culture which has changed much less in forty years than most cultures about which ethnographic films are made. But nevertheless, *The Moontrap* is one important model for what ethnographic films can achieve.

3. *The ethnographer's presence*. The very presence of outsiders, be they ethnographers carrying out their research, or filmmakers making films, inevitably has a myriad of influences on the people's behavior. Most ethnographic filmmakers in effect deny this and simply edit out any footage which reveals camera consciousness or too-blatant mugging. Admittedly, this is comparable to the model practice in ethnography, but it is one instance where the ethnographic practices can be followed too closely. The alternative is to build the outsider's presence into the structure of the film, to give some idea of how the people may be reacting to the outsiders, how questions are asked and answered, and the nature of deliberate intrusions, experiments, or the like which the outsiders are making.

Some ethnographic films make the anthropologist the major focus of the film. *Margaret Mead's New Guinea Journal* follows Mead in her return visit to Manus, forty years after her original fieldwork there. *Gurkha Country*, made by John and Patricia Hitchcock in Nepal, shows the Hitchcocks themselves living and doing research among the Gurkha. And *A Man Called "Bee": Studying the Yanomamö* presents the anthropologist Napoleon Chagnon at work in the Venezuelan jungles.

In fact, however, considering that the major use of ethnographic film is in introductory anthropology courses, it is surprising that there have not been more filmic attempts to show how anthropologists actually work. The success of written accounts of fieldwork like Claude Lévi-Strauss's *Tristes Tropiques* (1955), Kenneth Read's *The High Valley* (1965), and many others suggests that comparable films would be most welcome.

The most ambitious film in this vein was *Chronicle of a Summer* (1961), made by the anthropologist Jean Rouch and the sociologist Edgar Morin to capture the mood of Paris in the summer of 1960. Throughout the film, the two men are very visible and present. The film opens with Morin interviewing a young woman and directing her to do street interviews, asking people "Are you happy?" Morin and Rouch have several more talks with people, probing their psyches. Then, at a group discussion, Rouch announces that the film should turn to consider politics—Algeria and the Congo. More discussions with students, workers, and artists are followed by a sequence in a screening room where Rouch, Morin, and the subjects, who have just seen the film, discuss it, themselves, and each other. And finally, Rouch and Morin alone in the Musée de l'Homme, strolling past the relics of other cultures safely enclosed in glass, discuss whether they have shown the reality of their own culture in the film. *Chronicle of a Summer* is a richly provocative film in the extent to which it reveals the methodological mystery of ethnography, but as yet no other ethnographic films have risen to its challenge.

Nevertheless, there are various other ways in which ethnographic films have acknowledged and used the presence of the outsiders. In Adrian A. Gerbrands's *Matjemosh*, the narrator, supposedly speaking the thoughts of the Asmat (West New Guinea) woodcarver, tells of his wife's shyness before his friend, Gerbrands, and of his own amusement when Gerbrands asks him to make drawings of Asmat designs with a felt-tipped pen on paper for the film. (Unfortunately, since Matjemosh speaks in a Dutch-British accent familiar from a similar first-person film on Africa, the effect is somewhat lost.)

In *An Argument about a Marriage*, one of John Marshall's recently edited Kalahari Bushmen films, we are told that the conflict was precipitated when the Marshall expedition freed and brought back some Bushmen from enforced labor on a farm. And midway through the argument, when one man attempts to invoke the Marshalls on his side, the other replies, according to the subtitle, "Screw the Marshalls."

In *The Village* an interview technique is used. In some scenes Paul Hockings, the anthropologist sound man, is shown with microphone questioning the people, and villagers are often seen reacting to questions and remarks thrown out by Mark McCarty from behind the camera. In *The Nuer* an old man makes statements which seem to be responses to questions, although we never see or hear the questioner.

But there are many styles of ethnographic film, and some are better suited than others to including anthropologists in the film. It is always possible to explain the film crew's presence in written material which can be used to supplement the film, as, for example, the Rundstroms did in their essay on making *The Path*.

On the whole, the reasons in favor of showing the ethnographic presence in an ethnographic film seem to me to be compelling. In the first place, the ethnographic presence is, after all, part of the behavior being filmed, and so by including some of this in the film, we can see that part of the behavior and form some idea of how it affected the rest. In the second place, since the outsiders are mediating the information about one culture to an audience from another culture, including them in the film personalizes the mediation and, by making it more understandable, makes it more effective. The impersonal distancing effect of omitting the ethnographer decreases the ease with which an audience can understand a film; it also carries a political implication of noninvolvement, of treating the people as impersonal objects. This is a subtle matter, which I have thought about in regard to my own research. When I do research among the Dani, they are, inescapably, the subjects of my study but, I hope, not merely the objects I study and describe. Even when I quantify and generalize, I try not to lose sight of the fact that they are people who matter. Now, there are certainly ways to communicate this in films without showing the ethnographer, but the ethnographic presence is one way of adding this effect. (Of course, in making *Dani Sweet Potatoes* and *Dani Houses*, when I was both ethnographer and entire film crew, it would have been exceedingly difficult to have included myself or the effect of my presence in the films.)

There certainly could be drawbacks to the ethnographic presence in a film if, for example, shots of the ethnographer are included without concern for their relation to the action in the film. Obviously the idea is not merely to prove that an ethnographer and filmmaker were present, and to give them a chance to be movie stars, but rather to show the manner in which their presence was felt. There is sometimes a very thin line between the good and the bad uses of the ethnographic presence.

Selection and omission in the filmmaking process. The filmmaking process is one of tremendous selectivity. A camera is basically just a small box with a hole in one side, through which light passes to register an image on film.

Where the camera is taken, where it is set up, in which direction it is pointed, when it is turned on, all are decisions which form the first stage of selection. Then, in editing, another series of selections are made. These are all decisions which must be made fairly deliberately, and they result in a film which includes some behavior and omits other behavior. In all this, of course, film resembles ethnography.

1. *Point of view*. A film without a point of view is inconceivable. The selection and omission of the images which go into making a film must be based on some concept, or idea. Even if we imagine a film which is somehow constructed according to a table of random numbers, that film would be based on an obvious point of view. Dada as an artistic movement may have rejected "rules," but it certainly had a point of view.

The label "propaganda film" is often fixed on a film with a particularly obvious point of view, especially when the film's position is different from that of the critic. Rather than trying to define "propaganda film," let us shift to the more defensible and useful proposition that all films express *some* point of view. The points of view may vary greatly in substance, in the consciousness with which they were employed, and in the explicitness with which they are expressed, but they do exist and we can examine any ethnographic film in terms of them.

This seems quite obvious, but yet a fair amount of critical blood is shed over the question of whether or not films are "objective." Probably there will always be filmmakers who claim that they are just reporting the facts, just as there are ethnographers who would claim the same position. The university where I studied anthropology has for its motto the single word *Truth* (in Latin, of course). But for both ethnographers and filmmakers a more comfortable guideword would be *Truths* in recognition of the fact that there are many different approaches to understanding. In ethnography or in ethnographic film, it really comes down to this: selectivity is inevitable, and the author or the filmmaker should be aware of their points of view, since in the end they cannot avoid responsibility for them.

There are many points of view. Some films are made by special interest groups or subsidized by them with the explicit provision that they present the group's point of view. Basil Wright and John Grierson made *Song of Ceylon* for the Ceylon Tea Propaganda Board; the film consists mainly of poetic images of Ceylon, with some scenes of tea growing and preparation. Flaherty had engaged in the same very subtle imagery; *Nanook* was sponsored by Revlon Frères, a fur company, and one scene shows Nanook and his family at the company's trading post, exchanging furs for goods. Flaherty's

Louisiana Story was subsidized by Standard Oil, and it includes a shot of an oil well in the bayou. But it would be difficult to pinpoint ways in which these commercial interests shaped the point of view of the film.

On the other hand, *Radio Bantu*, produced by the South African Government Information Service, is very deliberately intended to create a favorable image for that country. Apartheid is pictured as a harmonious multiethnic society, focusing on the various Bantu language programs on the state radio. But the camera techniques themselves betray a very different handling of black and white individuals: whites are invariably in sharp focus, blacks almost always muted, silhouetted, or blurred by slick camera technique.

No Longer Strangers, made by the Regions Beyond Missionary Union about their conversion of the Western Dani to Christianity, is cinematographically rather crude, but very effective. It was made to show to church groups in the United States in order to publicize the Dani mission work, to raise money, and to recruit missionaries. The point of view is explicitly that of evangelical Christianity. Traditional Western Dani rituals are described as satanic mockery of Christianity. In other ways pre-Christian Western Dani culture is denigrated by such narration lines as "dancing girls perform their duties" and by the statement that the Dani had no tools, only stone axes. And while the narration describes the joys of the Western Dani when they became Christian, the visuals show masses of Christian Western Dani who are sullen, unsmiling, and not obviously joyful. *No Longer Strangers* makes an interesting counterpoint to *Dead Birds*. It was filmed near the Grand Valley, and the Western Dani of *No Longer Strangers* are (or were) closely related to the Grand Valley Dani of *Dead Birds* in language and culture. While audiences often react strongly to the point of view of *No Longer Strangers*, they rarely even recognize the much more subtle point of view which Gardner had built into *Dead Birds*. In fact, Gardner takes the usual anthropological position of accepting a culture's practices on its own terms. So Gardner discusses the Dani practice of cutting off girls' fingers as a funeral sacrifice and shows many mutilated hands; he shows and discusses war, battles, ambush, and killing without making a moral judgment. Of course, in my ethnographic writings about the Dani I do the same. But we must recognize that this amoral observation is as much a point of view as is the missionaries' condemnation.

Even *Dani Houses* expresses a point of view. It shows, with some respect, Dani housebuilding at a time when the Indonesian government is attempting to induce the Dani to change their house style on the grounds that traditional Dani houses are smoky and insanitary.

In addition to commercial, political, religious, and philosophical points of view, we must consider the scientific point of view, or the ethnographic inter-pretation. Just as ethnographic writings usually choose one sort of interpre-tation out of many possible ones, so do ethnographic films. However, films are more likely than writings to stay close to a straight descriptive level. Films like *Dani Sweet Potatoes* or *Dani Houses* do not undertake any real theoretical interpretation of Dani horticulture or construction. Some films use the native interpretation of events. For example, *Appeals to Santiago* used a first-person narration to describe the cargo ritual of the Chiapas Mayan and to present the explicit Mayan rationale that the ceremony is to honor the saints and has no economic function.

In the ethnographic tradition, the native explanation is an important datum, one which may agree with an ethnographic interpretation or which may be opposed to an ethnographic explanation. In *Appeals to Santiago* the Mayas explain the Chiapas cargo ritual as an expression of Christian piety and deny that it is a competitive prestige-seeking institution. Frank Cancian (1965) has analyzed the same institution from an economic standpoint, showing how it functions to even out wealth in exchange for prestige stratification. Neither the Mayans nor Cancian are wrong, but from one we hear the explicit or manifest function, and from the other an implicit, latent function. (And this hardly exhausts the possibilities, for other analysts could make other anal-yses.)

For example, in *Les Maîtres Fous,* Jean Rouch explains the Haouka cere-mony in psychological terms as a cathartic experience which releases hostility toward the colonial government and then allows the natives to return to their submissive daily occupations. In *The Turtle People*, Brian Weiss ex-plains Miskito Indian subsistence in ecological terms and argues that they are destroying the turtle population in return for short-term financial rewards but eventual economic disaster when the turtle boom is over. In *The Feast*, Asch analyzes a Yanomamö intervillage feast in terms of Marcel Mauss's gift exchange (Mauss 1925). The Rundstroms and Bergum show the Japa-nese tea ceremony in *The Path* in terms of its symbolic structure, and Susannah Hoffman in *Kypseli* analyzes the Greek village in terms of sexual division of labor.

Each of these films utilizes only one of several possible theoretical points of view to analyze a situation. But this is a legitimate ethnographic strategy, and the films cannot be faulted for not including all possible points of view. A legitimate criticism might be that they misused a type of explanation or that they chose an inappropriate type of explanation. But in any case, they are more ethnographic than a film like *Dani Sweet Potatoes*, in the sense that they attempt to move beyond ethnographic description to ethnographic explanation. This is also a more hazardous course, since it is much easier to make a satisfactory descriptive film than to achieve a film whose description *and* explanation are above attack.

2. *Technical distortions created by the filmmaking process.* Many sorts of distortions, selections, and omissions arise out of the basic technical steps of shooting and editing. The optics of the lens has an effect on perception of size and distance. For example, even though Robert Gardner filmed most of the battle scenes in *Dead Birds* with normal focal length lenses, they had the effect of foreshortening the scene, and so the front lines appear to be much closer to each other than they actually were. What are the ethnographic implications of this? Certainly Gardner's film sequences give a feeling for the movement of Dani battle that neither Matthiessen (1962), Broekhuijse (1967), nor K. G. Heider could capture in words. Yet, our printed words are carefully chosen, and, if they fall short of the film's holistic immediacy or fail in other ways to communicate what we mean, at least they are not betrayed by mechanical effects like the foreshortening distortion of a camera lens. The solution is not to reject film but to understand the distortions of cinema and make the necessary perceptual adjustments. A book like this cannot teach the reader to be able to correct for shots made with different kinds of lenses, but it can alert the reader to the fact that lenses distort visual reality in certain specific ways. And, even more important, written material accompanying films can specify where special effects, like telephoto lenses, have been used.

Editing for continuity. One of the most common conventions in film is to edit together shots of a single person or event which were taken at different times and places, in order to create the illusion of real continuity. My favorite example of this is the chase scene in *The Third Man*. The chase takes place in the old inner city of Vienna, where the chaser often loses his man as he cuts around a corner, finds him again, and then catches up, until finally the man disappears (into a sidewalk advertising kiosk, we learn later). The pacing of the scene is excellent and builds up excitement. However, I saw the film after I had lived in Vienna for a year, and it was a thoroughly disconcerting experience. Since street locations were chosen for the photogenic character and cutting was done without regard for geography, people race down one street, turn a corner, and are magically transported to another spot a mile away. Obviously *The Third Man* was edited for drama, and it cannot be used to make an accurate street map of Vienna.

But when this technique from fiction film is carried over into ethnographic film, it is not so harmless. Since we view ethnographic film as much for its true information as for its entertainment value, it does matter whether the continuity of a sequence is real or has been contrived in the editing room.

In ethnographic films there are countless scenes which have been created through editing. For example, when Nanook reaches his igloo in the blizzard and crawls inside, shots of a normal-sized igloo in a blizzard are followed by shots of the mock-up, half-shell, extra-large igloo taken on a clear day.

The giraffe hunt in *The Hunters* is edited together from scenes shot in different years with different men. If audiences could distinguish individual Bushmen—or even different giraffes—the effect would not be possible.

The major battle sequence in *Dead Birds* is put together from shots of different battles at different locations. Also, in *Dead Birds*, scenes of women going to the brine pool for salt alternate with scenes of men at battle, but in fact the brine trek was shot on a different day. All these are examples of distortions, but in each case editing is used to construct a description which is plausible. Before creating the counterpoint of men's battle and women's salt trek, Gardner was careful to determine that it could have happened. And it accurately illustrates the apparent indifference with which women did go about their normal activities while their men were engaged in battle.

This is a good moment in the argument to think some more about the nature of truth in ethnographies and in films. When I wrote this sentence I said relatively little, but what I did say was true: "Dani women never approach a battlefield, and in fact often work in the gardens apparently unconcerned, only occasionally looking up when a particularly loud cry comes from battle" (1970:111). If Gardner as a filmmaker wants to say the same thing in the visuals of a film, he is likely to have to say a great deal more, and not all of it can be literally true in the same sense. The women did go to the brine pool; the men did fight in several battles. But when he edits the footage from several battles together in order to say visually something like "this is what Dani battle looks like," or "this is the best picture I can give you of Dani battles," he follows the convention of filmmaking and lets the narration say, in effect, "this is one battle." So of course the audience sees it as one battle.

Then, he edits battle shots alternating with salt trek shots to communicate visually the idea that while Dani men fight, women do things like getting salt. But again, he follows film convention and claims in the narration that, on the day when that battle took place, these women went to the brine pool—and the audience sees it as an account of one particular Dani day.

Dead Birds is a particularly good film to use for this discussion because Gardner is so talented and knowledgeable as both a filmmaker and an ethnographer that we can assume he knew what he was doing. In his attempt to use the standards and conventions of both cinema and ethnography, he had to compromise, and he betrayed both to some extent. Now, a decade after *Dead Birds*, we can understand better what he did: in order to capture so many truths about the Dani, he had to tamper with the literal chronological truth in some points. But before we take a purist position it would be good to recall the discussion in chapter one about such cinematographic conventions in juxtaposition to the very comparable distortion that occurs in written ethnography.

Perhaps as we become more aware of these implications some anthropologists will come to reject the ethnographic films like *Dead Birds* in favor of more modest and literally true films like *Dani Sweet Potatoes*. This would be a shame, for the films in the grand tradition have their value as ethnographic and human documents. But we do have the right to insist that, if they are to be taken seriously as ethnography, their distortions must be explained and justified in separate written documents. The ethnographic companion to *Dead Birds* (Heider 1972b), written by Gardner and myself, is a step in this direction.

Real time and film time. Another common distortion in film is condensed time. Practically never does film time equal real time except, of course, within each individual shot. The actual time may be indicated visually or verbally. For example, in the narration of *Dani Houses*, I mention how long it took to build each structure. In fact, since the Dani work pattern is quite irregular, the time figures mean very little. But when I showed the workprint to audiences, they invariably asked for time data. So I provided these data, but more in the interests of relieving audience tension than for accuracy.

Most events shown in ethnographic films simply take too long to show in real time. Two exceptions occur in *An Ixil Calendrical Divination* and *The Path* (about a Japanese tea ceremony), both of which show short events in real time. It is interesting that most unprepared audiences find both films unbearably long, although they are only thirty-two and thirty-four minutes, respectively.

A few films use brief scenes in slow motion, or freeze frames, to point out complex behavior (as in *Trance and Dance in Bali*) or to dramatize a moment (as in *Dead Birds*). But I know of no use of time-lapse photography in ethnographic films (although ten years ago Robert Gardner talked about the potential of time-lapse photography in compressing a day's activity in a marketplace into a few minutes of film, in order to show general trends of activity).

THE SOUND TRACK

Synchronous sound. Although one tends to think of film as a visual medium, in fact nearly all ethnographic films have a sound track, and the relation of the aural to the visual is of great significance.

Technically, we can distinguish synchronous sound from wild sound. Synchronous sound is the sound recorded at the same time as the film was shot, with camera and tape recorder working in precise synchrony. Wild sound is any other sound: it may be of the same sort of behavior or plausible background noises, postsynchronized to the image to give the illusion of true synchronous sound; it may be a read narration; it may be mood music; it may be a mixture of several of these.

Ethnographically, synchronous sound is always desirable because of the way in which it reinforces the visual image. But until the mid-to-late-1960s, it was impracticable to make sound recordings in synchrony with the camera because tape recorders were too bulky, and it was too difficult to silence the noise of the camera machinery.

When synchronous sound includes speech in an exotic language, other problems arise which can be handled in various ways. Actually, much human use of language is so repetitive and so redundant with other sorts of behavior that speech can often be left untranslated and the audience really loses very little information.

This point is especially well illustrated by *Nawi*, a film by David and Judith MacDougall about the Jie of Uganda. Through most of the film the people are simply sitting around, doing minor tasks and talking a lot about very little. Bronislaw Malinowski coined the phrase "phatic communion" for this: ". . . flow of language, purposeless expressions of preference or aversion, accounts of irrelevant happenings, comments on what is perfectly obvious . . . a type of speech in which ties of union are created by the mere exchange of words" (1923:314–315). An occasional subtitle is enough to give us a sense of what is being said. *Nawi* is a rare attempt to capture the ordinary low-energy action so characteristic of most people much of the time.

An Argument about a Marriage and *The Feast*, both about high-energy events, use occasional subtitles in English so that the audience can follow the gist of an argument. In *The Nuer* and in *Rivers of Sand*, there are interview sequences in which, after someone makes a long statement in their own language, it is translated in the English narration. Direct dubbing of English, as is often done in commercial films, has not been tried with ethnographic films. The fact is that none of these alternatives are totally satisfactory. One wants to savor the experience of seeing and hearing someone expressing himself in his own language, and one also wants to understand what is being said. But except for the obvious perils of mistranslation, there are no major problems of misleading distortion in synchronous sound.

Cleverly postsynchronized wild sound is quite a different matter. All the sound in *Dead Birds* is postsynchronized and covers a wide range. For the most part, Michael Rockefeller, Gardner's sound man, tried to record wild sound to cover each shot which Gardner made. Then, when Gardner came to edit his footage, he could use the most appropriate passages from Rockefeller's tapes. But when I filmed Dani house construction and horticulture two years later, I did not attempt to record sound. (At that time I was alone with the Dani and could not face being sound man in addition to anthropologist and cameraman.) When I came to edit *Dani Sweet Potatoes* and *Dani Houses*, I decided not to go back to Rockefeller's tapes for appropriate wild sound because it simply wouldn't have been a close enough fit.

Narration. Narration consists of explanatory sentences read along with the visuals. It is almost impossible to have a narration which does not detract and distract from the visuals. Most ethnographic films show us totally exotic scenes: strange people wearing strange clothing doing strange things. Even if we focus our entire awareness on the scenes, we can barely take them in. But to have someone standing at our side telling us information in English as we are trying to watch the film must split our attention, and we lose much from both the auditory information and the visual scene. The purest solution to this problem was reached by the Netsilik Eskimo films, where there is no narration at all, only postdubbed natural sound. These films treat simple subjects lengthily and redundantly, and they are meant to be shown by instructors who can answer questions and direct students' discussions. Actually, much is clarified by the progress of the events themselves. But most ethnographic films must cover more activities less redundantly and are somewhat more self-contained. So narrations are almost inevitable, in some form or another.

Narrations vary tremendously, but much of the important variation can be summarized in terms of two dimensions. One dimension can be called "added information" and concerns the amount of information which the narration adds to the film beyond what is contained in the visual images; the other dimension can be called "visual relevancy" and concerns the degree to which the narration is relevant to the visual images. With these two dimensions, we can make a schematic diagram in which we can locate different narration styles.

At one end of the continuum is the banal redundant sort of narration, so typical of the worst "documentary" film, which tells us things which are perfectly obvious from the visuals. We hear "and the rains fell" as we see rain falling. This sort of narration is very closely related to the visual images but adds no information at all. A prime example of this style is found throughout

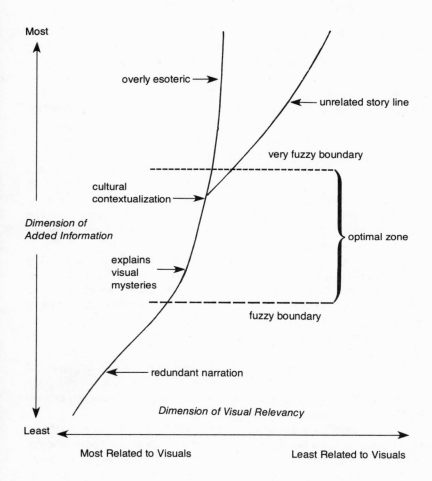

Diagram 1. A way of thinking about narrations or parts of narrations in terms of two attribute dimensions. The dimension of added information describes the amount of information in the narration which is not in the visuals; the dimension of visual relevancy describes the degree to which the information of the narration is directly relevant to the visuals.

the series of otherwise valuable films called the People of the Australian Western Desert. These films concentrate on technological processes, and most of the action is immediately understandable or is soon explained by the next actions. Nearly every word of the narration of all the films in this series is totally redundant with the visuals. At best, there are the proper nouns—names of people, of grasses, or of lizard species—which are really added information.

At the other extreme lies narration which is used to carry a story line when in fact the visuals show nothing of the sort. In some of the more exciting sections of *Dead Birds*, the excitement exists only in the narration, and the visuals are short, bland, scenic cuts. These sections are cinematically weak, but the narration is essential to carry the thread of the story while important events happened which could not possibly have been filmed. The amount of added information is very high, since the words have hardly any relation to the visual images.

Within the optimal zone in diagram 1 we can distinguish two styles of narration. In one, the words are used to explain or to clarify visual mysteries. In the other, the words put an act or event into the larger cultural context.

The two major misuses of narration, which fall outside the "optimal zone" on the diagram, are the low information redundancy and the high information overloading. The former is unnecessary; the latter could better be handled in printed form.

This scheme is fairly abstract. Applying its principle to criticism or to the making of a specific film involves a series of judgments which are often extremely difficult. For example, what is the line between necessary contextualization and overburdened esoterica?

At some points in *Hadza*, about a hunting and gathering tribe in Tanzania, the narration is more like a read ethnography which is only barely relevant to the visuals. It is as if, during these passages, the visuals were considered incidental illustrations for a written ethnography. Although visuals and narration do handle the same general topics at the same time, there is too rarely any real attempt to shape the narration around the specific events of the visuals.

Robert Flaherty, in his earlier, silent films, pushed the visual potential of film to the utmost by creating and then resolving mysteries visually. The Netsilik Eskimo series does the same, using carefully chosen wild sound without narration. A close comparison between the Netsilik Eskimo films and the Australian Western Desert series is very revealing. Both series were made in the mid-sixties, both about technological processes of a foraging group. The Netsilik budget was obviously much greater than the Australian budget, and the Netsilik films have excellent synchronized sound, while the

Australian films lack even wild sound. If the Australian films omitted narration, they would be essentially silent films, and silent films seem to be anathema to many. But since the Australian narrations add so little, they are, for all practical purposes, silent films. If one views one of them with the sound turned off—as I did once, by accident—it is clear how much more effective they are if one can really engage in the visuals, without the distraction of the narration.

An interesting question comes to mind: if the narration is so completely redundant with the visuals, it may be meaningless, but is it really distracting? Or perhaps, might it not assist viewers to concentrate on the visuals? This seems wrong to me. In the Netsilik films one is left alone and has to work to understand. I would say that this understanding will be much more real than if one had information prechewed, as it were. This question could easily be studied in an experimental situation where the same film was used with and without redundant narration to two different groups and then each group was tested to see which had learned the most from the film. (Throughout this book I am making a number of rather dogmatic assumptions about ethnographic film. They seem reasonable, but the next step is obviously to subject them to empirical testing.)

The Flaherty films, the Netsilik films, and the Australian Western Desert films all deal with technological processes, which are more amenable to a heavily visual clarification than are rituals. In films of rituals, where so much of the meaning is on the abstract, symbolic, verbal level, words are essential. In *Pomo Shaman*, the sparse commentary consists of statements by the shaman herself, recorded after the ceremony, describing what she is doing and how it felt to her. In Jean Rouch's films *Les Maîtres Fous* and *The Lion Hunters*, both dealing with complex ritual, a narrator gives what seems to be the native explanation of the different actions. Similarly, in *We Believe in Niño Fidencio*, the narration holds very closely to the participants' explanation of the rituals. In *Anasternaria*, the narration gives a frankly ethnographic, or analytical, view of the ceremony.

Both the native understanding and the analytical, ethnographic understanding are essential ingredients of ethnographic presentation. But there are real advantages in using the native view in the film and saving the ethnographic analysis for a written report. When the native statement is coupled with the native behavior, they reinforce each other and increase the immediacy of the film experience. The analysis is essential, but it is a removed line of thought and has the effect of distancing the viewer from the film.

In *Dani Sweet Potatoes* I tried to keep the narration down to an absolute minimum, using it only to explain actions which have been confusing or incomprehensible to an audience. And then, on Carroll Williams's advice, I laid each narration line in toward the end of a scene in order to engage the audience and give them time to be puzzled and, perhaps, to solve the mystery themselves.

In fact, the best solution seems to be the use of only synchronous sound, without any narration. The use of the printed ethnographic companion to films would relieve the narration of much expository burden. Then much background information could be printed, rather than narrated, and ethnographic filmmakers could concentrate on making their films more filmic.

Music. Music is inevitably a distraction except when it is sound which was actually happening when the visuals were shot, or, like the wild sound of the orchestra in *Trance and Dance in Bali*, is very appropriate to the visuals. The most common sort of music in ethnographic films is folksongs or instrumental music from the particular culture, but usually appearing in quite inappropriate contexts. For example, many scenes in *The Village* have background music, and, even though it is presumably authentic Irish country music, it strikes a false note. We see a long pan across a lonely landscape and hear lovely flute music, which sets some sort of mood, but we can hardly believe that a musician is or even might be present on the hillside. Even worse, similar music is heard over a scene of men struggling to build up a haystack. Stacking hay is hard work, but the music romanticizes it, and we certainly cannot believe that some village troubador plays for laboring men. The film elsewhere dwells on an English tourist who gushes over the picturesque primitive hand labor of the Irish countrymen, and most viewers understand clearly that such romanticism is in the eye of the beholder, not the worker. Yet, the filmmaker has done his own romanticizing by the use of the inappropriate music.

It may seem somewhat harsh to criticize such music, because it is undeniably pleasant, audiences enjoy it, and it fills in those silences which cinema convention has declared to be abominable. But the main criterion for ethnographic films should not be the quantity of information and impressions and sensory enjoyment they can convey, but rather how successfully they convey information. The primary criterion for a sound track should be that it reinforce the visuals by providing information which is very complementary, or that it at least be neutrally silent and not work in opposition to the visuals by introducing vastly new information.

FILM CONTENT

Holism and film. Although the holistic approach to human behavior is one of the hallmarks of anthropology, holism can hardly be called a theory. It is more of an attitude which characterizes anthropological research and distinguishes it from other sorts of social science research. It is reflected in the typical ethnographic research strategy of living in the midst of a society and making extensive observations of many events; and it is reflected in the typical ethnographic description, where the emphasis is on the interrelationships of many facets of a culture or a society. Ethnography places great emphasis on the context of behavior. Ethnography is extensive, in comparison with the more intensive interests so typical of sociological or psychological research.

The anthropological emphasis on holism accords very well with the capability of film to show things and events in physical and temporal context. But just as the mere fact of living in a culture does not guarantee holistic ethnography, so merely shooting film does not assure holistic ethnographic film. There are some basic anthropological principles, or corollaries of the principle of holism, which are directly pertinent to the problems of ethnographic film. They have to do with contextualization of behavior and what we can call whole people, whole bodies, and whole acts.

1. *Contextualization*. Contextualization is a basic but easily misunderstood concept or imperative. At one extreme it is obvious: things or events must not be treated in isolation; they have meaning only in context. On the other hand, it is clearly impossible to describe everything about everything. But it seems safe to say that although no film (or ethnography) has been hurt by overcontextualization, many are flawed by inadequate contextualization. The precise degree of contextualization which should be achieved in an ethnography or a film is, in the end, a matter of judgment.

One can speak of contextualization in terms of cultural aspects, or in more physical environmental terms. As an example of the cultural aspects, I have often heard *Dead Birds* criticized for its lack of attention to Dani women. This is really the common but veiled complaint that the critic wanted a different film. While *Dead Birds* focuses on Dani men's life, it actually does show many aspects of women's life in the gardens, getting salt, and at ceremonies. But the film is about Dani men, and in Dani society the women are peripheral to the political, ritual, and warfare activities which concern the men.

In *Dead Birds*, Gardner has used early shots very skillfully to establish the context of the landscape in which the action will take place. He used several long shots made from a hill. First, in a long pan following a hawk which glides across the landscape, actually below the camera level, the bird is in focus and the landscape out of focus. But the narration at this point is very dense and important, so the audience is allowed only an impression of the landscape. This shot is followed by another, also from the hilltop, which begins looking down into Weyak's village, then pans along a path to the gardens, then zooms out to a wide-angle view of gardens, no-man's-land, enemy country, and the far mountains; a later shot from the same high vantage point also begins at Weyak's village and follows another trail out to Weyak's watchtower. Thus economically and dramatically and very visually, we are put into the Dani physical world.

The Nuer, in contrast, lacks such landscape contextualizing. Of course, in the flat Nuer country the filmmakers had no handy hilltop. And they may have felt that to use shots made from airplanes or helicopters would have been obvious and intrusive and would have destroyed the delicate ambience of their film. But ethnographically the necessity for this sort of contextualization—for example, showing a complete Nuer village, showing the cornfields, or showing the relationship of village to fields to pasture to river—should override other considerations.

In other respects The Nuer shows many acts taken out of context, presumably for aesthetic but not ethnographic reasons. Grass is another classic case of decontextualization, for we see at great length the dramatic march of the Bakhtiari herdsmen over the mountains of Persia to their summer pastures, but we learn practically nothing of the social, political, or economic context of this movement. It exists as a brilliant, isolated, act.

Mokil, which deals with overpopulation on a Micronesian atoll, and Rivers of Sand, about sex roles in an Ethiopian tribal society, are particularly notable attempts to handle the complexities of these topics through film. Taking overpopulation or sex roles as the central fact, each film explores the ramifications and implications of that fact in a meandering, often repetitive, but quite contextualized fashion.

At the other extreme is the short film which deals intensively but not contextually with a single narrow subject. An excellent example of this is the thirty-three–minute film on the Kwakiutl with the strange title Wooden Box: Made by Steaming and Bending. The film shows a master craftsman making a wooden box. It is a fascinating tour de force, but, without other knowledge of Kwakiutl woodworking and symbolism, the viewer has no way of understanding the context of that act.

2. Whole bodies. One of the most entrenched conventions of cinema is the full-face close-up, in which a person's head or even just a face fills the entire screen. The close-up is remarkable on several grounds, the first of which is its unnaturalness. In normal interaction a person may focus visually on another person's face, but only if the two faces are very close to each other

will the face be the *only* thing present in the total visual field. Even in cultures where normal conversational distances are relatively short, the eyes of a normally sighted person can visually attend to more than just the face of another by means of peripheral vision and quick eye shifts. A close-up shot of a face does not permit this. As an extreme example, when two people are in sexual embrace, their faces may be so close that their actual visual fields approximate that of a cinema close-up shot.

But interestingly enough, in such scenes in films where close-ups of faces might be experientially real, close-ups are rarely used, and the camera stays far enough removed to get at least full head-and-shoulder shots. One can accept the proposition that close-ups are perceptually and logically unnatural, but the fact is that they are conventions of film, accepted and expected by filmmakers and film viewers alike.

The real question here must concern their effect on the ethnographicness of a film. We begin with the obvious fact that every close-up frame of a face means a frame omitting the rest of the body. What, then, are the gains and losses of this particular selection? One argument in favor of close-ups is that they create visual variety and so sustain the viewers' interest. But this argument is based on the assumption of fairly low audience commitment, and I think that it is worth trying to encourage a new way of seeing ethnographic film.

A second argument in favor of the close-up is that film should be allowed to examine parts of a body, or whatever, one after the other in close-up detail in the way that a written account does. But this argument misses the point of a difference between words and film. In order for words to describe an entire body at once, they must move to a very general level. No single word or phrase can describe the details of hands, face, body, and voice. Rather, each must be dealt with in turn, as a kind of isolating close-up. But a film image does hold so much information that a long shot of a person's body can, in fact, allow the viewer to observe hands, face, body, and voice in simultaneous interaction.

A third, more important argument is that full-face close-ups allow the audience to experience and relate to a person. This assumes that the core of the persona is best visible in the face and can be understood through the face. If this is valid, it depends on the fact that the close-up cuts out everything but the face and is not based on the absolute size of the image of the face. Films using facial close-ups are viewed on screens and television tubes of widely varying sizes, with viewers sitting at various distances from the image. So the actual size of a face's image, measured in degrees of retinal image, varies greatly from that for a person who sits close to the screen in a large theater to someone who sits across the room from a small television set. There is certainly some perceptual principle at work here, but I know of no studies of it. I think that it is clear that size of image is less important than limit of information. Close-ups are a convention not because greater size of facial image is desirable. On naïve grounds one might say that if that were so, people would sit in the front of movie theaters rather than toward the rear. Instead, close-ups are used because they concentrate attention on the face and give relatively greater detail. But what is lost when the bodies are omitted? A great deal. It is clear that from an ethnographic standpoint much specific communication is done through the body, and much general cultural information is contained in body movement.

Recent research on nonlexical or nonverbal communication has shown the importance of the body in modifying, supplanting, and even contradicting those purely verbal messages which had so long been the sole focus of interpersonal communication research (cf. Bateson 1972:228–243; Birdwhistell 1970:173; Condon and Ogston 1966; Ekman and Friesen 1969a, 1969b). Ironically, the loss of communicative behavior through the use of facial close-ups is a relatively small loss in most ethnographic films, since so few even attempt to capture interpersonal communicative behavior.

But the loss of whole body movements in general is important. Alan Lomax and his associates at Columbia University, who have been carrying out choreometric research on dance and work motion, have shown that there are definable styles of motion which vary from culture to culture and culture area to culture area. Lomax's research has made us aware of the profound cultural significance of movement itself and what can be called the cultural integrity of the whole body. In terms of ethnographic film, it means that the entire body must be observed and photographed and that filmmakers must be exceedingly cautious about moving closer than whole body shots (Lomax 1973).

There are countless examples in ethnographic films where the camera moves in on faces (or isolates other body parts) and prevents us from seeing what is happening in the rest of the body. In *Holy Ghost People*, a film about an Appalachian Pentecostal church, there are frequent scenes where people enter ecstatic trance states. Their ecstasy is obviously felt and expressed in their entire bodies, yet the camera compulsively zooms in on faces. In *Desert People* and the other films of that series, the facial close-ups prevent us from following the rhythm of whole bodies and even, at times, from seeing the technology of what the whole bodies are doing. The loss of this information is hardly compensated for by the close-ups of expressionless faces, often shot from above so that we do not even have a good view of the face itself.

In *The Nuer*, some of the most effective scenes are long shots of people walking alongside their cattle. One is able to see the exotically graceful ways in which these tall thin people walk and how their walking seems so in harmony with the movements of their cattle. But in the same film we are not allowed to watch the movements of women pounding maize in wooden mortars as the women stand, rhythmically thrusting the long wooden pestles into the mortars. After a brief establishing shot, the camera plays in and out on moving body parts: upper arms, breasts, and faces. The camera creates its own vision. It is reminiscent of contemporary "underground" filmmakers who use footage of childbirth or other real events to create a personal aesthetic pattern. This approach can result in an interesting film, but it makes little sense to judge such a film by the standards of ethnographic reality.

It is probable that the information loss is not so critical when the people and the activity in the film are familiar to the audience. Then viewers can reconstruct entire acts from minimal cues. But in most ethnographic films, which show exotic acts from exotic cultures, viewers need all the information they can get, and the deprivation of information in the close-up is particularly felt. A counterargument could be made to the effect that the increased detail of a close-up shot of a face gives more information, not less, and in addition, creates a mood of intimacy between viewer and subject which is lost when the camera stays back at the necessary distance to capture images of whole bodies. Although these counterarguments are interesting, they do not seem convincing. But certainly the whole matter should be investigated by empirical research.

The question comes down to this: Is the ethnographic filmmaker to focus on the events of the film, or on the conventions of the cinematography? It is very difficult for a creative filmmaker to resist the conventions of the craft. But respect for the subject demands a limit on such conventions and creativity. The words "creativity" and "imagination" must not be allowed to become points of false debate, however. The creativity and imagination essential to good science, here including ethnographic film, are significantly different from the creativity and imagination essential to good art, here including most other uses of film.

It is not possible to make absolute rules like "whole bodies must always be in frame" or "close-ups are always bad." But generally speaking, close-ups should be avoided unless they really contribute to picking out details which are lost in the whole, and then close-ups should be preceded and followed by contextualizing whole shots. This principle holds for close-up shots of technical processes as well as of body parts. I do not want to condemn all close-up shots, but I do want to insist that the close-up should be seen as an extraordinary step, taken only because of extreme necessity.

A nice illustration of this turned up in two thirty-minute videotapes shot by two different students for an ethnographic film course at UCLA in 1974. The subject of both tapes was the same: a father helping his four-year-old son assemble a jigsaw puzzle. Both filmmakers had the same goal, which was to show the interaction between the two. One tape showed both actors in full frame throughout; the other moved in and out, to the father's face, then to the boy's face, then to the boy's hands, and so forth. The second tape was more aesthetically pleasing, but the first showed much more about the interaction. Filmmakers judged the second more interesting and complained at being asked to watch through a stationary lens for thirty minutes. Anthropologists judged the first more revealing about the father and son interaction. Both, in their own terms, were right.

The concepts of "contextualization" and "whole bodies" are different ways of getting at the ability of film to present simultaneously occurring events simultaneously, allowing the viewer's eye to travel back and forth, examining parts and the whole. Word descriptions may attempt this holism, but it is hindered by the inexorable linearity of words strung together in sentences.

3. *Interaction in context*. One of the most consistent absences in ethnographic films is any description of communication or other sort of interaction between people. In part this is because normal, naturally occurring conversation is so hard to film. It is a relatively low-energy, fragile sort of behavior, which is easily disrupted by the camera. It is much easier to film one person or many people engaged in some physical activity. So the percentage of real interaction in any ethnographic film is very low.

And when filmmakers do shoot conversation, they usually ignore the more basic fact: conversation is interaction. The work of Gregory Bateson, Ray Birdwhistell, and others, such as Adam Kendon, have shown how much a conversation between two people is not just a sequence of utterances. Rather, both parties are communicating constantly about a variety of things. At any one moment, a person may not be speaking words, but is nevertheless contributing to the interaction. This is ignored in the usual film or television drama, where conversations or interactions are often filmed as an alternating series of full-face shots of people talking and reacting. In drama it may have its uses: by reducing the communication to a minimum, all attention is crudely and powerfully focused on verbal and (occasional) facial channels. But of course, it results in the loss of the great range of communication nuance of real life.

Alan Lomax has pointed out (in a personal communication) how well the richness of this range is captured in a final sequence in *The Hunters*, where one hunter relates the story of the hunt to others of his camp. The camera keeps its distance, so we can not only see the vivid act of storytelling, but we can also appreciate the dynamic role of the audience. A strikingly similar scene was used twenty-five years earlier in the Eskimo film *Wedding of Palo*, when Samo tells a group of people how he chased and killed a polar bear. One could argue that both these scenes are too visually complex to be understandable. Indeed, it is only after repeated viewings in slow motion that one can really appreciate the complex coordination of narrator and audience.

One of the few attempts to make a film about a conversation is John Marshall's Kalahari Bushman film, *Joking Relationship*. The entire fifteen minutes of the film show the casual banter between a man and a girl. The two are relatives, and their relationship is such that they are not permitted to marry, but they are allowed an informal, even bawdy "joking relationship" (Lorna Marshall 1957). This film is an extremely interesting attempt to capture the mood of this particular kinship tie, and, thanks to a good sound track and subtitles, it is quite effective. But through most of the film the camera moves back and forth in a series of close-ups. Only rarely are the two people shown at the same time. We see one person and then the other. In fact, we hardly see a relationship in the literal sense. The behavioral interactions were created in the editing room. The film is a testimony to how much skillful editing can gild over faulty camera work.

So far we have dealt with attributes which are essentially technical and cinematographic, though with ethnographic implications; now let us turn to matters of film structure and content, which are more directly ethnographic.

4. *Film structure*.

Flaherty is always considered a master storyteller, and some of his films reflect this. Although there is little storytelling in *Nanook*, he does realize a story in *Moana*, where the Samoan youth achieves manhood and wins his girl by undergoing the tattoo initiation ritual. In *The Hunters*, John Marshall tells a story of hunger, and how the Bushmen track the wounded giraffe for days in order to kill it and bring back meat for the camp. In *Dead Birds* Gardner is able to create a story by following the events of war for the five months he was in the Grand Valley, as Weyak's group lose a boy to the enemy but finally restore a balance by killing one of the enemy.

Some films, like the Netsilik Eskimo series or *Dani Sweet Potatoes*, achieve a continuity not through the adventures of an individual but by following a technical process to completion. The weakest attempt at a story line, but one which ethnographic filmmakers often try, is "a day in the life of the village." James L. Gibbs, Jr., and Marvin Silverman's film of the Kpelle of Liberia, *Cows of Dolo Ken Paye*, started out in this way, but partway through the filming they stumbled on to a dramatic legal case which became the subject of a quite different and much more focused film (see below, under "Beginnings").

Bateson and Mead achieve another sort of continuity in their Balinese films by filming a few individuals, especially infants, over a long period to show the developmental process. *Karba's First Years* is a unique ethnographic film which traces the development of a Balinese boy through the major stages of early childhood. Few anthropologists studying child development have designed their research to actually follow individual characters as they grow up, and no one else has ever tried to show this on film.

Many ethnographic films are little more than series of vignettes, or "impressions." *The Nuer* is this sort of film: brilliantly filmed impressions of a cattle camp. An occasional event is stumbled on: a marriage dispute, a mass healing ritual, an initiation, and an exorcism. But the filmmakers did not know enough of the culture to know what should be filmed in order to show complete and understandable event sequences. The prototype of the impressionistic vignette film is *Song of Ceylon*, made by John Grierson and Basil Wright for the Ceylon Tea Propaganda Board in 1934. It is a series of scenes, loosely organized into thematic sections.

A film may be thought of as having various levels, of possibilities for continuity. The entire film may have a single theme, like *Dani Sweet Potatoes*, which follows the Dani horticulture sequence from clearing land through planting, weeding, and harvesting, to cooking and eating. Practically every shot in the film contributes to that complex.

On a less inclusive level, a film may contain one or more shorter activity sequences. Edited throughout *Dead Birds* is a complete sequence of women producing salt, and another of a man knitting a shell funeral band. The overall story of *Dead Birds* is the accident of the sequence of events during five months in 1961. But if Gardner had not had the overall story line, he would still have had a film of several reasonably complete shorter event sequences. A major fault of *The Nuer* is that, despite its aesthetic photography, it has practically no complete story or continuity on any level. It remains a series of fragments—lovely, but ethnographically unsatisfactory.

Whole acts. A sort of holism which cinema is ideally suited to present is process, or behavior through time. But in order to show the structure of a whole act, especially in nonstaged shooting of naturally occurring behavior, one must know how to anticipate an action. Acts have beginnings, peaks, and endings. The unknowledgeable observer or filmmaker will notice an act only at its peak, will not have enough experience to know that it will happen soon enough to pick up the beginning and will not have enough sense of the act to follow it past its end. An especially telling film is Hugo van Lawick's *Baboons of Gombe*. Van Lawick has been filming primates, especially chimpanzees, at Gombe Stream Reserve in Tanzania for a decade. With his experience, van Lawick is able to follow a variety of acts, large and small, almost from before they begin, through their peaks to their endings.

The criterion that whole acts are desirable refers to the selective use of structural features of the act. It is not possible to demand that everything about an entire act be shown. This is unrealistic realism. Two ethnographic films have attempted to approach this by having film time equal real time. But even in these films much had to be omitted. In Carroll Williams's *An Ixil Calendrical Divination*, the camera holds in close to the hands of the diviner as he lays out his pieces on a surface. Consequently, we do not see the interaction between the diviner and his patients, an interaction which surely gives the sensitive diviner as much information about the problem as the way in which his pieces fall on the board. In *The Path*, the Japanese tea ceremony is shown in real time, but in order to film it the action was stopped and repeated many times, and so a part of the interaction between hostess and guests was lost to the film. It is conceivable that a short and simple act could be filmed by several cameras simultaneously and then projected on multiple screens. This would be an interesting exercise. But it would merely be the reproduction of reality, not the understanding and analysis of reality which is the basis of ethnology (or any other science).

Selection of shots is inevitable in filmmaking. The criterion of whole acts demands that the selection be done so as to present the important features of an act. Just as there are many different legitimate ethnographic approaches, so the selection may bring out different aspects of an act. It is not good to be dogmatic at this point. The Rundstroms selected shots in *The Path* to show yin-yang balance and energy management (Rundstrom, Rundstrom, and Bergum 1973). Other anthropologists might make quite different selections from the same event.

The whole act must be adequately represented by selective elements. And in this context, where we are speaking of the ethnographicness of film, we can say without hesitation that the selection should be done on the basis of some ethnographic understanding, and the adequacy of the whole act can be judged ethnographically.

In *Dani Sweet Potatoes* and *Dani Houses*, I deliberately planned to show each step of the sweet-potato cycle and of construction. In *Dead Birds*, Gardner follows the entire salt-making process and all the major steps of a funeral (as well as we understood them in July 1961). In contrast, the initiation sequence in *The Nuer* is a sadly incomplete document. It shows a few peak moments, dwelling at length on the bloody forehead incisions. The film captures the most obvious events, but what it omits (presumably because it hadn't been filmed) are many important symbolic events which we know of from the ethnographic literature; and, presumably, from ignorance of the meaning of initiation itself, the film doesn't even follow the individuals into manhood.

A major weakness of Frederick Wiseman's 1974 television film, "Primate," was that, although he spent one month shooting and two hours of screen time on bits of scientific experimentation at the Yerkes Primate Research Center in Atlanta, the film never followed a single experiment as a whole act. This approach had interestingly different effects on different viewers. Laymen (including television critics) were simply horrified by the picture of senseless butchery in the guise of science; one friend of mine who is familiar with that sort of research could fill in the gaps for himself and was fascinated by the film; more thoughtful viewers reacted strongly against the film itself on the grounds that it made no attempt to communicate an understanding of primate research by presenting whole acts, but only used scenes of gore to play on the audience's emotions and turn them away from such research.

a. Beginnings. We can consider the wholeness of any act in terms of its beginning, its peak, and its ending. The beginnings are the most difficult to film because this really demands enough knowledge of the behavior to anticipate an act before it begins. In some acts, such as trance states, the transition from the previous, or "normal," stage into the altered state is of obvious importance. Trance is an extreme example, but it serves as a good model. When we speak of "an act," we mean some relatively definable behavioral event which is different from what preceded it and from what follows. If one is writing ethnography, it is easy to construct sentences after the fact which will describe the beginnings of an act. But it is much more difficult to have a camera at the right time and the right place to capture an act as it is beginning.

One ethnographic film which does this particularly well is Cows of Dolo Ken Paye, made in a Kpelle village in Liberia by Marvin Silverman and James L. Gibbs, Jr. The major act in the film is the resolution of a conflict over a cow which had been found in a farmer's field, was wounded by a machete blow, and died. The peak action began with the discovery of the wounded cow, and following the case from that moment was relatively easy. But thanks to Gibbs's intimate ethnographic understanding of the culture, the film was able to recreate the beginning of the act. It described the complex implications of rich men's cattle and poor men's farms; it incorporated still photographs which Gibbs had taken of a similar conflict years earlier and which had served as a precedent, and it even was able to include serendipitous footage of the culprit chopping a log with his machete, taken before the act. Thus, with the combination of luck and deep ethnographic understanding, the film was able to anticipate an act. The beginning of the act was approximated in the editing room, in a manner similar to the ex post facto written description of an ethnography. It may well be that this sort of reconstructed beginning is all that we can expect for many larger acts shown in ethnographic films.

   b. *Peaks.* Peak activity is that part of the act which involves the most energy and activity and draws the most attention. It is this peak activity which even the most unknowledgeable filmmakers can capture. But there is a great danger of infatuation with peaks. Just because peaks are so obvious to see and easy to film, attention is distracted from other activity which may be less energetic but, in cultural terms, more important. John Heider (1974) has discussed this in human potential encounter therapy, where a peak, or "blowout," is customarily followed by a long plateau of creative ecstasy. He describes how, in the early days of Esalen Institute, group leaders were preoccupied with achieving the peak experiences. Only gradually did they come to understand the importance of the postcathartic plateau. In ethnographic film, a similar preoccupation with peak drama can make for an exciting but superficial picture of an event. But I feel diffident about accusing specific films of this failing, since the full ethnographic facts are usually not available.

   c. *Closure.* The final part of the demand that ethnographic films show whole acts is the demand that they achieve some degree of closure: that acts or events are brought to some sort of completion.

   We are familiar with the conventional symbols of closure which cinema adopted from storytelling: the boy and the girl live happily ever after. A more cinematographic symbol of closure is the final shot of a sunset, preferably over an ocean. The power of the symbol is that we accept it as closure and feel satisfied. This is a kind of emotional satisfaction, different from the intellectual need for complete information.

   In *The Nuer* we are often brought into an important event, and, before we learn its outcome, the subject is changed. In *Dead Birds*, on the other hand, Gardner's final philosophical statement about the Dani and death is a very personal attempt to give emotional closure to the entire film, probably for Gardner himself as well as for the audience.

   Many ethnographic films do impose a punch-line structure. This is the structure of the joke which closes with a climactic punch line. But in fact, most behavior does not follow this pattern. It may reach a peak, or climax, but then slowly fades out into another act. Two of John Marshall's Kalahari Bushman films have particularly fine treatments of closure. In *The Hunters*, after the giraffe has been killed, we follow the bringing home of the meat, the distribution, and the eating. Then it is all recapitulation as one of the hunters tells the story of the hunt, and, when that is over, people slowly get up and disperse. In *Bitter Melons*, the final sequence shows men doing a dramatic ostrich courting dance. The final shot seems to hold forever as the men drop the dance, lie down to nap, or drift away. Still the shot holds, as two boys make a half-hearted attempt to revive the dance. Then they, too, become still. And finally, after all activity has slowed down to a stop, the shot is over. To hold a shot so long takes courage in shooting and courage in editing (edited by Frank Galvin). But *Bitter Melons* achieves an exceptional degree of closure through it.

   d. Density of information. The criterion of whole acts is one way of judging whether or not a film presents an adequate amount of information. From that perspective, a film which adequately shows an entire act has an adequate amount of information. The whole-acts criterion is a structural criterion, since it assumes that we can talk about a basic and necessary structure to behavior, the elements of which must be shown in film.

   But we need another criterion which specifies the pure load of information presented in a film. It is quite possible for a film not only to show structurally excellent whole acts but also to have too much information. This is a danger to which ethnography is not subject. An article or a book can be made longer and can be broken up with chapters and subchapters. No one is forced to read an ethnography book straight through at a steady pace in one sitting. In fact, tables of contents and indexes are invitations to dip selectively. But films are designed to be seen without interruption from the beginning through to the end. Few people have the inclinations, the equipment, or the opportunity to use films like books. One compromise has been the shot-by-shot analysis section of the Ethnographic Companions to Films modules (e.g., K. G. Heider 1972b), which in effect translates the film shot-by-shot into the printed word and thus makes it available for convenient re-viewing.

   The old joke about the book which told the little boy more than he wanted to know about penguins takes on a different meaning here. The boy could easily escape by not reading parts of the book. But if he had seen a film which presented more about penguins than he could understand, he would have a valid complaint.

   One way in which a film can have too much information is a sort of non-ethnographic paradox, as in the initiation sequence of *The Nuer*. Not enough of the initiation is presented to make it understandable. Yet in another sense there is too much of the inadequate information. By this I mean that the film has created visual mysteries which go unexplained either in the visual or the aural channels of the film.

One might also argue that any film contains too much information. For someone like Ray Birdwhistell or William Condon, whose research on micro-behavioral data demands countless intensive viewings of a few frames of film, even twenty minutes of film, seen once at twenty-four frames each second, would be a painfully intolerable overdose of information, no matter how ethnographic the film. But the data of microbehavioral analysis must be distinguished from the grosser sorts of information which ethnographic films are designed to communicate. So it is legitimate to say that a film may have too little, too much, or appropriate amounts of information, depending on the audience.

This overloading of information is especially common in ethnographic films made by anthropologists. It seems reasonable to blame this on the anthropologists' familiarity with print where, as we have seen, more informa-tion can always be added in another (often unread) chapter or appendix, in such a way that it does not compromise the entire work. Most of the criteria discussed in this chapter are ethnographic criteria; the danger of information overload is one that cinematographers are much more sensitive to than are most anthropologists. The problem is to judge how much infor-mation is enough, and to stop there.

The most usual and obvious locus of superfluous information is, of course, in the narration. I now think that I did this in *Dani Sweet Potatoes*. Since I had no sound other than the narration, I was self-conscious about having too much silence. Also, after showing a work print of the film to many differ-ent sorts of audiences, I was very aware of the sorts of questions which were usually asked, and I tried to use the narration to head them off. So, for example, over a shot of a large newly planted sweet-potato bed, I de-scribed the other sorts of gardens and cultigens of the Dani. Now in fact, that information is available in print, and the view of the garden in itself, without narration, contains enough information to engage an audience. So here and elsewhere in *Dani Sweet Potatoes* the narration provides an over-load of information.

Information overload can result from a narration which says too much, visuals which show too much, or from a combination of narration and visual excesses. But this is a particularly difficult judgment to make. Much depends on the nature of the audience and the intensity with which the film is viewed. If an ethnographic film is shown on prime-time television to a mass audi-ence, it can tolerate far less information than if it is only to be studied by advanced college classes in anthropology, who may see it more than once.

Particularizing and generalizing. One of the greatest differences between words and pictures lies in the fact that words are necessarily abstracted generalized representations of reality, while photographs, in contrast to words, and despite the subjective selection involved in shooting, are in some sense direct, specific representations of reality. But ethnographers not only use words, they also use words to make generalizations, to state cultural norms. However, the strategy of ethnography is to begin with the data of specific behavior and to move to the cultural generalization. And a good part of any ethnographic writing is description. It is in the realm of the critical anecdote, or the illustrative case, that film most often serves ethnography. Film shows a specific event, carefully chosen and edited for its ethnographic import, and put into a generalizing framework by a few words printed in a title or read in the narration.

So most ethnographic films make cultural generalizations by showing a particular event or artifact or person and implying or openly claiming that the particular is typical, that is, general. Thus, in *Dead Birds*, we are invited to see Weyak and understand "adult Dani men"; we see Weyakhe's funeral and understand "Dani funerals." Whether this is a justified step depends greatly on the filmmaker's understanding of the culture and skill at choosing shots which are indeed fairly typical. But obviously behavior varies so much that no one man or single funeral can really be representative for all men or all funerals. The ethnographic filmmaker has an obligation to select reasonably representative events, but also to provide, perhaps in the film, and certainly in supplementary written material, those ethnographic data which will spell out the relation of the specific image to the range of variation of those specifics and to the general.

These thoughts raise an interesting question: how far *can* films go in making general statements out of specific raw material? It is obvious that this can be done with generalizing words read in a narration. But how much can it be done visually?

Douglas L. Oliver, in his monograph on the Siuai of Bougainville, said that his photos would give a better idea of Siuai physique than his words could (1955:10). So ethnographic films which show dozens or hundreds of people in a society can provide the raw materials for generalization. In *The Nuer* this is done quite deliberately in several sequences which show a dozen or more short shots of ivory bracelets, or tobacco pipes, or scarification designs. Thus, although one photograph or twenty-four photographs per second can never actually make a generalization, a film can show a range of acts, events, or artifacts and so set up a generalization. In terms of film language, or semiotics of film, we can think of two different sorts of visual implications or statements: in one, a single representation is shown and a generalization implied, for example, "this is how Weyak behaves and therefore how Dani men behave." In the other, we see many different representations, and the implied statement is "here is how *x* hundred Dani men appear and therefore the range of similarity and variation of Dani men."

For the most part these unspoken "statements" are merely filmic implications and are not really comparable to explicit, mutually understood intentional linguistic utterances. To some extent the filmmaker intended to make them, and to some extent some viewers perceive them, but there are always ambiguities: one can legitimately ask, "What did he say?" and "Is that what he really meant?" Such ambiguity may be used to great effect in art, and indeed, it may be considered the essence of art. But it is not tolerable in science. So we must insist that ethnographic filmmakers clarify in narration or in writing the extent to which they mean generalizations to be made.

One of the films in the desert people series (part two, *Gum Preparation, Stone Flaking; Djagamara Leaves Badjar*) does this well, taking particular pains to warn us when it would be false to draw the logical generalization from the visuals. At the beginning we are told that the films were made in an unusually dry spell, certainly an important factor on the Western Desert of Australia. Elsewhere we see a man perform a task but are told that usually women do it; we see a bark dish but are told that most dishes are made of solid wood; and as we see a man getting gum from grasses, we are told that this time he is having particular difficulty in making the gum congeal.

Whole people. It is safe to say that all ethnographic films show people, even though few are actually about people. But the extent to which individuals are identified and shown as well-rounded personalities varies greatly. Some films show only faceless masses, while others make the viewer acquainted with one or two individuals. There is no single ethnographic standard. Although the goal of ethnography is some sort of generalized cultural or social statement, there are many different strategies of research and description. This is reflected in ethnographic films made by ethnographers themselves. Some, like Adrian Gerbrands's *Matjemosh*, show us much about the life, work, and even the thoughts of one New Guinea woodcarver. The film is similar to Gerbrands's book (1967), which explores Asmat art through a detailed description of six different carvers. At the other extreme we find Brian Weiss's *The Turtle People*, shot while Weiss was doing research for his dissertation in ecological and economic anthropology at the University of Michigan. Weiss's film very much reflects his concern for the impersonal impact of outside economic factors on the culture and the society of the Miskito Indians of Nicaragua. Now, one could argue that *The Turtle People* is just as humane as *Matjemosh* in terms of being concerned with real problems of people. But its strategy is not to focus on any individual Miskito.

Films made by nonanthropologists are as varied along this dimension as are those made by anthropologists. However, there is the strong Flaherty tradition of building a film around a single person. Robert Flaherty began this with *Nanook* in 1922, and followed it through his other films. However, the more I see *Nanook*, the less I feel that the film really tells us much about Nanook as a whole person. Perhaps much of *Nanook*'s reputation came from a few shots where Nanook engagingly smiles or laughs into the camera lens. But, despite these reservations, there is no question that Flaherty led both naïve audiences and film critics to relate directly and warmly to the Eskimo man as a whole person.

So there is precedent in both ethnography and ethnographic film for a wide range of treating or ignoring individuals. But I think that we can argue, as much on filmic grounds as on ethnographic grounds, for whole people rather than faceless masses.

Semiotics. Semiotics, or semiology, has gained currency recently as a general cover term for a wide range of interests which have developed out of linguistic concerns. One of these interests concerns the way in which cinema resembles language. A language is a system of symbols used to communicate; a film uses symbols to communicate. But the crucial semiotic question focuses on the "system": Does a film or do films embody regular systems which are in any sense comparable to syntax or lexica? Put another way, do the concepts of syntax and lexicon help in understanding film? The idea is fascinating, but I do not intend to deal with it at any great length here. Much of this work has been done in French and is only gradually being translated (e.g., Metz 1974).

Sol Worth, in his 1969 paper "The Development of a Semiotic of Film," explores these sorts of questions: Is there a grammar of film; if so, is there a possibility of "ungrammatical" film statements? But Worth is careful not to claim too much. The experiment with Navajo filmmakers which Worth carried out in collaboration with John Adair attempted to explore some of these implications: if there is something analogous to a language of film, will Navajos make films in some sort of Navajo film language which is different from other (English/Hollywood/etc.) film languages?

But as yet there is very little in the way of results that one can point to with any degree of confidence. At present the differences between film and the language of ordinary discourse seem more important than the similarities: language is a more precise, instrumental medium of communication; film communicates, of course, but in a more diffuse, noninstrumental way. The utterances of language are brief, and reaction and correction are immediate,

usually measurable in seconds; with film, if there is any comparable message turn-around time, it is measured in months and years. Film may be
more analogous to novels or plays. But even there, while novels and plays
are constructions of the language of everyday discourse, the ingredients of
film (shots and sequences of shots) are not present in ordinary discourse of
any sort.

But despite these problems and uncertainties, we can point to some
general principles.

1. *Cutaway shots.* The juxtaposition of two shots often implies that the
contents of both are related. When a shot of a face watching something
off-camera is followed by a shot of a logical Something, it is almost inescapable that the filmic statement be read, "X is watching Y." A very common
cinematographic technique using this is the cut-away, when shots of an
event are broken by close-ups of people's faces supposedly watching the
event. The cut-away has special perils for ethnographic film.

First, the cut-away is often used to break up a long action, on the assumption that the audience cannot tolerate focusing its attention on a single act
for more than a few seconds. But in fact it is more likely that in ethnographic
film we need to see a long and uninterrupted act and that the editor's decision to cut away will be based on some arbitrary number of seconds and will
do violence to the integrity of the action. (A slightly more excusable use of
the cut-away is when the camera has stopped or run out of film, and the cut-
away is a sort of rescue operation.)

Second, the shots inserted as cut-aways are usually shot before or after
the main action. Then, when they are inserted into the sequence of an
action, they are likely to be misleading. If the main action is a vehement
speech or the peak moment of a funeral, for example, we understand the
cut-away to mean something to the effect that "this is how X was observing
and reacting to this moment in the speech or the funeral." Such cut-aways
could be literally true if two cameras were being used in synchrony with each
other. If not, the cut-away is more or less false. It has only aesthetic rationale
and adds nothing of ethnographic value. I would go further and say that the
ethnographic demand for a longer, uncut shot would be more aesthetic,
despite its cinematographic unconventionality.

2. *Camera angle.* A very common practice is to shoot down on people. In
my experience most ethnographic filmmakers are taller than most people
being filmed. When cameras are hand-held, or tripods are set up, it is usually

at comfortable standing height for the filmmaker, but, especially in close-ups, this results in the camera and the viewer looking down on the people. Now, one can talk about the meaning of camera angle. Specifically, let us imagine three close-up shots of a person, showing just head and shoulders —one at his eye level; one from above, looking down on his face; and the third from below, looking up into his face. Each of these three shots would have somewhat different connotations. One of the important dimensions of meaning which vary here has to do with superiority/inferiority, status, and personal distancing. Of course, the English words appropriate to the situation reinforce this suggestion: specifically, that a shot from above, or a film which consistently shoots from above, is in some way making the viewer superior, looking down on the people who are beneath him. This is one factor in what can be called the semiotic of film. It seems certain that continuous use of high camera angle results in greater distance, less empathy, and so perverts what is presumably one goal of ethnographic film.

THE AUDIENCE

Intended audience. Printed anthropology is generally written with a specific audience in mind: reports of research and theoretical contributions are presented in journal articles and monographs aimed at professional colleagues; textbooks, prepared for students, are secondary reworkings of description and theory; and, occasionally, anthropologists write popular accounts in such journals as *Natural History* or in books aimed at a general lay audience. These are not absolute categories, for journal articles are reprinted in readers for courses, and monographs may be also used in courses; an occasional textbook like Eliot D. Chapple and Carleton S. Coon's *Principles of Anthropology* (1942) may also be an important theoretical formulation; and series like the Holt, Rinehart and Winston Case Studies in Anthropology are short ethnographies written for classroom use and may be the only comprehensive reports on particular cultures. But on the whole, writers have fairly specific ideas of their primary audience and adjust their writing to the appropriate level.

Most ethnographic films, on the other hand, seem to have been made with little thought for any specific audience. The outstanding exception is the Netsilik Eskimo films, which were carefully designed for a primary-school audience. During the planning stages a team of educational specialists, led by the psychologist Jerome Bruner, worked out a program for using ethnographical materials to introduce basic social science. They decided on the specific concepts which they wanted to communicate to a specific audience and then produced films which would best accomplish this.

Film demands on the audience. The range of demands which film can make on an audience is nicely demonstrated by the old and new versions of *Nanook*. Flaherty originally made *Nanook* with various visual puzzles which heightened a viewer's awareness while he tried to understand what was going on, and then rewarded the viewer by showing him the outcome. The revised version of *Nanook*, however, introduces explanatory narration and soothing music. The viewer now is disengaged and merely relaxes in the wash of sight and sound. There is little left to be attentive to. The narrator attends to all.

We have already discussed how easy it is to overload a film, especially through the narration, with so much information that viewers simply cannot comprehend it all. The most obvious sort of overloading is to read great quantities of information in the narration.

Another way to overload a film is to lead viewers to a level in the action which is simply too complex to be grasped in a film. The new Marshall Bushman film, *An Argument about a Marriage*, is overloaded in this way. If viewers were only to see the film as an argument, there would be no problem. But the filmmakers wanted to make the viewers understand the historical background and present course of a fast-moving argument involving the complex Bushman marriage practices. No viewer can keep up. Film simply cannot carry so much information. Even if a film is designed for a high level of complexity, there are bound to be questions which can only be answered in written accompaniments.

Perhaps *The Path* makes more demands on an audience than any other ethnographic film. It was designed not just to describe the Japanese tea ceremony but to reproduce its qualities so that audiences could use it almost as a meditation, or study experience. At the other extreme, Flaherty made his films for a general theater audience and probably had no thought that one day they would be seen almost exclusively in classrooms. The Bateson and Mead Balinese films are the closest approach to a filmic monograph, and certainly they were conceived as an integral part of a monographic report.

But for the most part, ethnographic films apparently try to appeal to all audiences. (One must say "apparently" since the filmmakers' aims are rarely accessible.) There are some advantages to this approach. It does give a film a chance at several different markets. But this may be illusory. In fact there is basically only one market for ethnographic films: the educational or classroom market. This market uses films as much for entertainment value as for informational, educational value. There is a sort of positive feedback at work. Films are entertaining, so they are used for entertainment. And so most anthropologists have not considered the serious anthropological potential of film. (An important exception to this is in the study of primate behavior. Since E. R. Carpenter's films of monkeys in the 1930s, primate films have been important scholarly productions.)

It is probably fairly easy for a filmmaker to state, if pushed, the audience which he had in mind for any particular film. But I think that for most filmmakers this is an ex post facto rationalization. To the extent that they have an audience in mind, it is a select preview audience of their friends.

A more interesting question concerns the attributes of ethnographic films which are made for entertainment or for instruction. The major differentiating dimension is the intensity of information. Films like *Nanook*, or *The Nuer*, contain relatively little information, but give much atmosphere; films like *Childhood Rivalry in Bali and New Guinea*, or *Dani Sweet Potatoes*, are loaded with information and spend little time on pure atmosphere.

In my experience of showing ethnographic films to school teachers I have been surprised at the resistance to films which show "naked savages." Nakedness is culturally patterned, of course. The Dani are extremely modest, in the sense that they do have some body parts which must be covered, and they are quite embarrassed if these should inadvertently be exposed. But to most American audiences, naked breasts of mature women, or scrotums of mature men, constitute nakedness. And school teachers strongly resist using films which show peoples whose patterns of body coverage differ from their own. The teachers say that their pupils are too immature to see such films without making jokes, or that the parents would object. As an anthropologist, I accept this as an accurate appraisal of at least parts of contemporary American culture. It is undoubtedly very fortunate, and perhaps no accident, that the major curriculum film project for grade schools was made on the Netsilik Eskimo, a fully clothed people.

Credibility. For me one of the most baffling and subjective attributes of ethnographic films is credibility, or believability. For years I have been showing ethnographic films to audiences of many different sorts, and I am still surprised at what people will or will not accept. Much of the narration in *Mosori Monika*, which was shot in Venezuela, comes verbatim from statements made by a Warao Indian woman and a missionary nun. These statements were translated into English and read by people with slight accents. Chick Strand, the filmmaker, obviously tried hard to create a sense of the two conflicting realities, that of the Indians and that of the missionaries. But to my surprise, many viewers think that the entire narration was created out of Strand's imagination.

A somewhat more understandable, but equally unjustified disbelief greets *The Turtle People*. The beginning titles establish the Miskito Indians as living in Nicaragua. Most viewers know that Nicaragua is Spanish-speaking, but practically none know that the Miskito actually speak English, not Spanish. So, when we hear heavily accented English in a first-person native narration, it is difficult to believe that it is genuine. Perhaps in these films, some explanatory introductory titles could help. If people would believe the titles.

Earlier, I questioned the convention of the ethnographic present in ethnographic films. But for some viewers this convention allows them to believe. Many viewers are disturbed by the asphalt highway which appears in the background of some shots of Peter Furst's *To Find Our Life: The Peyote Hunt of the Huichols of Mexico*. In fact, the Huichols do now use vehicles in their peyote quest, and some of their sacred spots are beside highways. It would be much more logical if Furst's honesty had strengthened the credibility of his film, not weakened it. In reporting these reactions, I may seem to undermine the previous arguments for explicit reality. Of course that is not my intention. In fact I have no idea how representative are the doubters I reported on, and I should expect that, as viewers become more sophisticated, their credulity will become better placed.

THE FILM AND THE ETHNOGRAPHY

The extent to which the film is informed by the ethnography. In this chapter we have discussed many attributes which contribute to a film's ethnographicness. But underlying all these considerations is a single one: an ethnographic film must be based on ethnographic understanding. The more successfully a film has this understanding, the more ethnographic it will be. However, this is no simpleminded recipe like "stir in heaping spoonfuls of ethnography . . ." If that alone were sufficient, we could turn over all ethnographic filmmaking to ethnographers and be assured of successfully ethnographic films. But in fact, a film may be made by an informed ethnographer and still be a failure ethnographically. In making an ethnographic film, ethnographic understanding is useless unless it is transmuted by filmic imagination. But despite these cautions, the single best predictor of ethnographicness in a film is the extent to which an ethnographer was involved in the filmmaking.

The basis for this has already been discussed at some length in chapter one: in ethnographic writing, the understanding and conclusions emerge through the process of data gathering, analyzing, writing, and rewriting and are constantly being refined and even changed up to the very moment of publication; but in filmmaking, on the other hand, the initial act of shooting footage produces fixed images and so precludes much of the rewriting possible in ethnography. The result is that whatever ethnographic understanding can be applied to the film must be present beforehand.

The best model for ethnographic filmmaking is *The Feast* (see chapter two, "The New Bushman Films") where the filmmaking began only after the ethnography was completed, and the film itself was made by a filmmaker (Timothy Asch) working in the field in close collaboration with the ethnographer (Napoleon Chagnon). In this way there is maximal opportunity for the fully digested ethnographic understanding to shape the film. Other films, such as *Dead Birds*, *Dani Sweet Potatoes*, and *Childhood Rivalry in Bali and New Guinea*, were shot by ethnographers as research was underway, and so do have considerable ethnographic input.

Relation to printed material. No ethnographic film can stand by itself. An ethnographic film must be supplemented by written ethnographic materials. Or, put the other way around, an ethnography is a written work which may be supplemented by film. It is easy to conceive of ethnographies which are words without pictures. In fact, most of the best ethnographies either have no pictures at all (especially in the case of journal articles) or have a few irrelevant snapshots. But it is impossible to conceive of ethnographies made up of pictures without words. Of course, ethnographies can be complemented by pictures. And the use of film to describe some things which words cannot describe is one of the major challenges of ethnographic film and is discussed in chapter four.

But the ethnographic enterprise demands a depth of description and of abstract generalization which cannot be handled in pictures alone. And while a few words can be spoken as narration, they are inadequate to convey much, and in any case are so overpowered by the visuals that they are barely understood.

So an important criterion of the ethnographicness of any ethnographic film is the extent to which it is backed up by written material. One major purpose of the catalogue *Films for Anthropological Teaching* (K. G. Heider 1972c) has been to list the ethnographic materials relevant to the various films.

For some films, like *Grass* or *Tidikawa and Friends*, there are as yet no ethnographic materials, and so the films are not very useful ethnographically. There is just too much unexplained mysterious action. Most films have some vaguely relevant literature, but there has been little or no direct coordination between film and literature. We may be able to learn a little about the culture, but probably nothing about the filmmaking itself.

The first satisfactory film in this respect is *Dead Birds*, which is accompanied by considerable literature about the Dani, the culture in the film, and especially by an "ethnographic companion" (K. G. Heider 1972b), a short pamphlet which specifically ties the film in to the ethnographic literature. More such study guides are beginning to appear, and they will greatly increase the ethnographicness of the films which they accompany. In addition to the ethnographic companion for *The Path* (Rundstrom, Rundstrom, and Bergum 1973), there is the major program of study guides being produced on the Marshall Kalahari Bushman films (see Reichlin 1974a–g; Marshall and Biesele 1974; and Reichlin and Marshall 1974) and on the Yanomamö films.

The Attributes as Dimensions

The previous discussion has treated a number of principles which underlie any consideration of the ethnographicness of film. These attributes can now be considered as continua or attribute dimensions, along which the various films can be placed. While it would not be sensible to treat any of the attribute dimensions as finely calibrated scales, it is possible to present them as qualitative scales. For ease of discussion, and in anticipation of the composite attribute dimension grid to follow, the more ethnographic values of each attribute dimension will be placed on the right end of each scale, and a few representative films will be used as examples of the different values along each scale. The reader will soon notice that although many films are used as examples, only three films are used for every attribute dimension. These are *Dani Sweet Potatoes* and *Dani Houses*, which I made, and Robert Gardner's *Dead Birds*, with which I assisted. I have used these three films extensively because I know them more intimately than any other films. But the purpose of the attribute dimensions is to present a systematic way of judging any ethnographic film, and I hope that the reader will not hesitate to use the attribute dimension diagrams as a sort of notebook, or tally sheet, on which to enter comments on other films, whether they are ethnographic or not.

Table 1

Basic Technical Competence	distracting incompetency	reasonable competency	exceptional quality

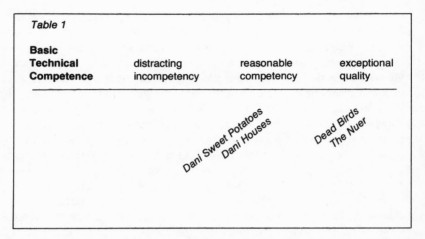

The attribute of basic technical competence refers simply to such cinematographic features as focus and exposure. If a film is too deficient in this attribute, it will not be distributed and, if screened, will be incomprehensible and misunderstood. It is obviously an advantage for a film to be of the highest technical quality. Films like *Dead Birds* and *The Nuer* are certainly above average in this respect. Some films, like *Dani Sweet Potatoes* and *Dani Houses*, show lower technological competence but are still usable.

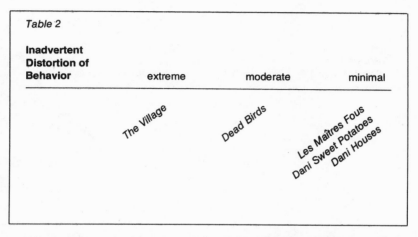

Table 2

**Inadvertent
Distortion of
Behavior**

	extreme	moderate	minimal

The Village — extreme

Dead Birds — moderate

Les Maîtres Fous
Dani Sweet Potatoes
Dani Houses — minimal

The presence of a camera team is bound to have some effect on behavior. No matter how unobtrusive the filmmakers attempt to be, there will be some inadvertent effect on the behavior. The two major factors in this inadvertent distortion are the degree of camera consciousness, resulting in unease before the camera, and the relative energy levels of the camera crew and the subjects. In *The Village*, the filmmakers tried to capture the casual interaction of the Irish villagers, but they constantly drew attention away from the interactions toward the camera itself. At the opposite extreme, the possession ceremony in *Les Maîtres Fous* or the battles and funerals in *Dead Birds* had such high levels of energy of their own that the filmmakers were virtually ignored.

Although the activity in both *Dani Sweet Potatoes* and *Dani Houses* was at a comparatively low energy level, the people were not at all camera conscious, and they were so familiar with the filmmaker that there seems to have been little inadvertent distortion of behavior. It would be possible to use footage of such distortion and incorporate it into a film so as to make a telling ethnographic point. But when distortion is unintentional, uncontrolled, and unincorporated into the ethnographic understanding, it detracts from the ethnographicness of the film.

Table 3			
Intentional Distortion of Behavior	extreme	moderate	minimal
	Netsilik series The Path	Dead Birds	Dani Sweet Potatoes Dani Houses

The behavior shown in a film may have been intentionally altered or distorted by the filmmaker in a wide variety of ways which range from altering the material culture to staging, triggering, or reconstructing behavior. One can speak of this as a variable running from extensive to minimal intentional distortion of behavior, but it does not necessarily correlate with ethnographicness. There can be good ethnographic justifications for any degree of such distortion. One cannot say that the Netsilik Eskimo films, with their reenactment of Eskimo life, or *The Path*, in which the Japanese tea ceremony was filmed bit by bit, are less ethnographic than *Dani Sweet Potatoes*, which was filmed with no intentional distortion of behavior. In each film, distortion was made or avoided for legitimate ethnographic reasons.

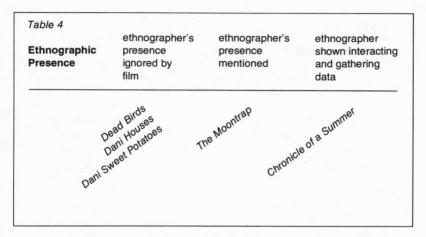

Table 4

Ethnographic Presence	ethnographer's presence ignored by film	ethnographer's presence mentioned	ethnographer shown interacting and gathering data
	Dead Birds *Dani Houses* *Dani Sweet Potatoes*	*The Moontrap*	*Chronicle of a Summer*

By judiciously incorporating the ethnographer into the film, as part of the behavior being recorded, a film can become more self-conscious about the sorts of information which it communicates. Jean Rouch has been the leading (and almost the only) practitioner of this approach. His *Chronicle of a Summer*, which is not simply about Paris in 1960 but more about how an anthropologist and a sociologist go about investigating Paris in 1960, illustrates the strengths of using the ethnographic presence. *Dead Birds* and the two short Dani films, on the other hand, omit the presence of the ethnographers completely. In the middle ground is *The Moontrap*—although we never see the filmmakers, we are told that the revival of whale trapping, which is the subject of the film, was done at their instigation.

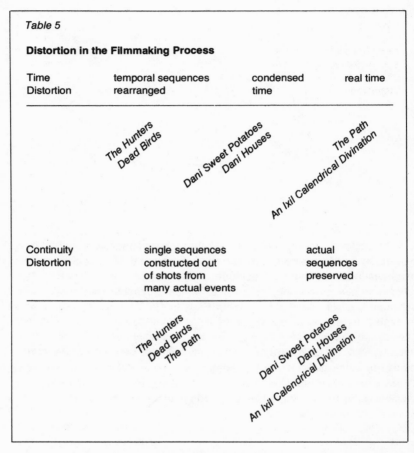

Table 5

Distortion in the Filmmaking Process

Time Distortion	temporal sequences rearranged	condensed time	real time

The Hunters / *Dead Birds*   *Dani Sweet Potatoes* / *Dani Houses*   *The Path* / *An Ixil Calendrical Divination*

Continuity Distortion	single sequences constructed out of shots from many actual events	actual sequences preserved	

The Hunters / *Dead Birds* / *The Path*   *Dani Sweet Potatoes* / *Dani Houses* / *An Ixil Calendrical Divination*

Time, continuity of action and place, and perspective are just some aspects of reality which may be intentionally altered in the process of shooting and editing film. For convenience, we can talk about these in terms of only two variables, time and continuity. Some films are high on one, but low on the other, like *The Path*, which presents the Japanese tea ceremony in real time but using shots which were made separately and then edited together for continuity. *An Ixil Calendrical Divination*, on the other hand, was made in real time and shot at a single divination ceremony.

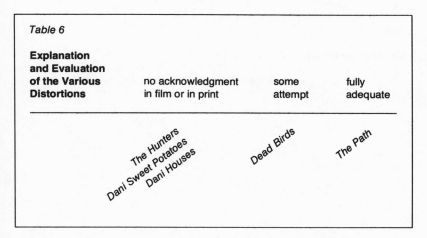

Table 6

Explanation and Evaluation of the Various Distortions

	no acknowledgment in film or in print	some attempt	fully adequate
	The Hunters *Dani Sweet Potatoes* *Dani Houses*	*Dead Birds*	*The Path*

In the course of filmmaking, a vast number of changes, intentional as well as inadvertent, are wrought on reality. Some of these are quite necessary, desirable, and intentional, others not so. But it is crucial to the ethnographicness of a film that they be explained, justified, and evaluated. This criterion could well be taken to ridiculous extremes: it would be impossible to explain every frame of every shot. But the filmmakers and ethnologists should spell out in reasonable detail how they made the film. The bulk of this has to be done in print, through something like an ethnographic companion or study guide which can accompany the film. The fullest example of this explanation and evaluation is *The Path*, which is accompanied by a detailed publication written by the filmmakers themselves (Rundstrom, Rundstrom, and Bergum 1973). *Dead Birds*, with its ethnographic companion (K. G. Heider 1972b), is fairly well analyzed from this standpoint, while *The Hunters*, *Dani Sweet Potatoes*, and *Dani Houses* have not yet been dealt with in any detail (all three are discussed throughout this book, of course, and ethnographic companions or study guides are planned for all).

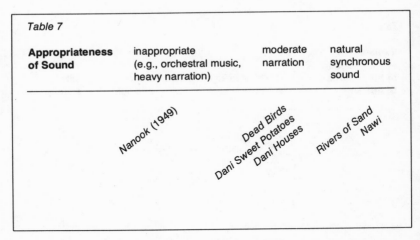

Table 7

Appropriateness of Sound	inappropriate (e.g., orchestral music, heavy narration)	moderate narration	natural synchronous sound

Nanook (1949)   Dead Birds   Dani Sweet Potatoes   Dani Houses   Rivers of Sand   Nawi

The appropriateness of sound may vary greatly from scene to scene within a film, as in *The Village*, which has both the synchronous sound of the Irish villagers' conversation and inappropriate flute music accompanying haying scenes. The extreme in inappropriateness was reached in the 1949 version of *Nanook*, which has both full orchestra and a wordy, redundant narration. Both *Nawi* and *Rivers of Sand*, on the other hand, use almost exclusively natural synchronous sound.

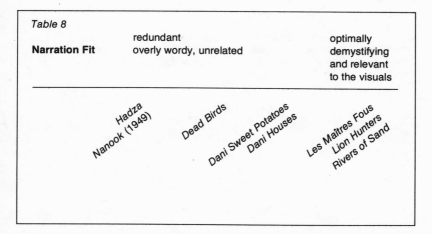

Table 8

Narration Fit | redundant overly wordy, unrelated | optimally demystifying and relevant to the visuals

If narration is used at all, it is best when sparse and very closely related to the visuals, explaining or adding only minimal information needed to demystify behavior which cannot be explained visually. Redundant banal comments which add no new information ("the rains fell" sort of statements) are often used simply to fill the air with words, as was the case with the 1949 sound version of *Nanook*. In films made in the late 1950s and early 1960s (like *Dead Birds* and *Hadza*), before synchronous sound was possible, narrations were overly wordy and attempted to convey masses of ethnographic information which had little basis in the visuals. In the films by Jean Rouch, like *Lion Hunters* and *Les Maîtres Fous*, fairly wordy narrations were used to explain and translate those symbolic aspects of ceremonies which simply could not be elucidated in a purely visual manner. In *Rivers of Sand*, the sound track is mainly synchronous sound, with only a few explanatory lines of narration.

Table 9 **Contextualization**	isolated behavior shown out of context	gestures toward contextualization	well contextualized
	The Nuer	_Dani Houses_ _Dani Sweet Potatoes_ _Dead Birds_	_Rivers of Sand_ _Mokil_

Contextualization is a measure of the degree to which a film sets behavior in its cultural and physical context. Of course, no film can make a complete contextual statement. And in some senses a short single-concept film may be contextualized not by itself but by other similar films (as the new Bushman films are) or by written materials (as with the two shorter Dani films).

Table 10

Whole Bodies	excessive fragmented close-ups	maximally necessary whole bodies

The Nuer
Holy Ghost People

Dani Sweet Potatoes
Dani Houses
Trance and Dance in Bali

In nearly every case, long camera shots which include whole bodies of people in frame are preferable on ethnographic grounds to close-ups of faces and other body parts. An occasional close-up which can show otherwise obscure detail is useful, but most ethnographic films thoughtlessly overemploy the close-up shot. Among the few films which resist the abuse of the close-up and tend to keep actors in full frame are *Trance and Dance in Bali* and *Dani Sweet Potatoes*, both filmed by anthropologists.

Table 11		
Whole Acts	fragmentary bits of acts	beginnings, peaks, and ends of acts

Primate
The Nuer

Dani Houses
Dani Sweet Potatoes
Dead Birds

Cows of Dolo Ken Paye
The Hunters

Ongoing naturally occurring behavior can be analyzed and understood as a series of acts, of greater or lesser magnitude, many occurring simultaneously but often not coterminously; and each of the acts has a beginning, a peak, and an end, not to mention precedents and consequences. Some ethnographic films, like *Cows of Dolo Ken Paye* and *The Hunters*, are particularly successful in portraying whole acts in this sense of the concept, while films like *The Nuer* and *Primate* are made of poorly understood fragments of behavior.

Table 12			
Whole People	only faceless masses		develops feeling for an individual

The Turtle People   *Dani Houses* *Dani Sweet Potatoes*   *Nanook* *Dead Birds* *Matjemosh*

Although the printed word inclines written ethnography toward generalization, the specificity of film makes it easy and desirable to show a few individuals as whole people with real personalities, rather than merely members of faceless masses. *Matjemosh*, *Dead Birds*, and *Nanook* all explore cultural phenomena by focusing on the lives of one or two individuals. There are no advantages in shooting only faceless masses, and a film like *The Turtle People*, by identifying no individuals, loses some impact.

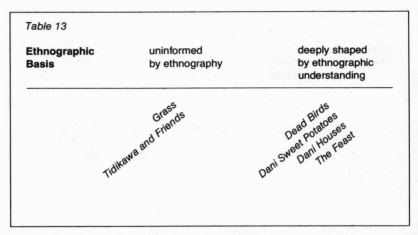

Table 13

Ethnographic Basis	uninformed by ethnography	deeply shaped by ethnographic understanding
	Grass *Tidikawa and Friends*	*Dead Birds* *Dani Sweet Potatoes* *Dani Houses* *The Feast*

The degree to which an ethnographic film has been informed by ethnographic understanding is difficult to determine with real confidence, but one obvious indicator is the role (if any) which an ethnographer had in the filmmaking. Some films, like *Dead Birds* and *The Feast*, were made as part of an ethnographic study. At the other extreme are *Grass* (on the Bakhtiari of Persia) and *Tidikawa and Friends* (on the Bedamini of Papua New Guinea), both remarkable films in their own way, made by keen observers, but quite uninfluenced by ethnographic understanding.

Table 14		vaguely	fairly well	fully
Relation to	no	relevant	supported	integrated
Printed	printed	printed	by printed	with printed
Materials	materials	materials	materials	materials

Tidikawa and Friends   *Grass*   *The Nuer*   *Dani Sweet Potatoes* *Dani Houses*   *The Path* *Dead Birds*

The degree to which an ethnoghraphic film is supported by written materials about the culture and about the circumstances of the filmmaking ranges from *Grass* and *Tidikawa and Friends* (for which there is some casual material on the filmmaking but no ethnography), to *The Nuer*, for which there is ethnographic material on the culture but from a different time and place; to *Dani Sweet Potatoes* and *Dani Houses*, for which there are published materials on the subject of the films by the filmmaker-ethnographer, to *Dead Birds*, for which there is extensive ethnography and a study guide.

The Attribute Dimension Grid

A final step in the systematization of these attributes which determine the ethnographicness of film can be taken with the use of a synoptic attribute dimension grid (see K. G. Heider 1969). So far the discussion has examined one attribute after another, using various films as examples of the different values of each attribute. Now we can make up an attribute dimension grid, which will allow a profile of ethnographicness to be drawn for any particular film. The attribute dimensions have already been formulated with the more ethnographic values toward the right. They were first presented in a more or less logical order, but now they must be rearrranged in order of their importance as a measure of ethnographicness. This order is a particularly crucial step in the whole argument. I certainly do not claim to have established a perfect immutable order of importance. On the other hand, the order is not at all random, for its logic emerges from the preceding discussion.

The attribute dimensions, arranged in order of their ethnographicness, are shown in diagram 2. The attributes toward the top of the diagram are those which are most crucial, for if they are neglected the ethnographicness of a film is most seriously compromised. Those attributes toward the bottom are less crucial in the sense that they have more acceptable values, or degrees of freedom. For example, the first attribute, the degree of ethnographic basis of a film, is extremely important for its ethnographicness. But films may fall at many points along the last attribute, intentional distortion of behavior, and still be very ethnographic.

It is always dangerous to the health of any such exposition to become as specific as this, for it opens up the door to countless attacks on countless details. Certainly some details could be changed without affecting the main purpose, which is to develop a systematic set of criteria for ethnographic film.

Ethnographic Basis	uninformed by ethnography		deeply shaped by ethnographic understanding
Relation to Printed Materials	no printed materials	vaguely relevant printed materials	fairly well supported by printed materials	fully integrated with printed materials
Whole Acts	fragmentary bits of acts		beginnings, peaks, and ends of acts
Whole Bodies	excessive fragmented close-ups		maximally necessary whole bodies
Explanation and Evaluation of the Various Distortions	no acknowledgment in film or in print	some attempt	fully adequate
Basic Technical Competence	distracting incompetency	reasonable competency	exceptional quality
Appropriateness of Sound	inappropriate (e.g., orchestral music, heavy narration)	moderate narration	natural synchronous sound
Narration Fit	redundant overly wordy, unrelated		optimally demystifying and relevant to the visuals
Ethnographic Presence	ethnographer's presence ignored by film	ethnographer's presence mentioned	ethnographer shown interacting and gathering data
Contextualization	isolated behavior shown out of context	gestures toward contextualization	well contextualized
Whole People	only faceless masses		develops feeling for an individual
Distortion in the Filmmaking Process: Time Distortion	temporal sequences rearranged	condensed time	real time
Continuity Distortion	single sequences constructed out of shots from many actual events		actual sequences preserved
Inadvertent Distortion of Behavior	extreme	moderate	minimal
Intentional Distortion of Behavior	extreme	moderate	minimal

Diagram 2. The attribute dimensions, arranged in order of their ethnographicness. The more ethnographic values of each attribute are toward the right.

The profiles for individual films can be plotted onto a skeleton attribute dimension grid, as in diagram 3. There I have made profiles for *Dead Birds*, *Dani Sweet Potatoes*, and *Dani Houses*. A blank attribute dimension grid is provided in diagram 4, and the reader is invited to use it as a work sheet and plot out profiles for other ethnographic films.

The attribute dimension grid provides a convenient summary of the basic ethnographic attributes of a film. Finally, it answers in a simple way the complex question which I rejected in its naïve form on the first page of the Preface: "What is ethnographic film?" We can now respond in terms of the profile: The further to the right on the grid the profile remains, the more ethnographic is the film. This entire chapter, trying to specify what ethnographicness in film means, is summarized by the right-hand values of each attribute dimension.

But I want to emphasize most strongly the limitations of the attribute dimension grid. It is not the Complete Automatic Ethnographic Film Critic, capable of resolving all film arguments in a single page. It is a guide for analyzing and describing the ethnographicness of a film. But much is left out, including some attributes discussed in this chapter, which, although they are important, are not critical to ethnographicness. For example, the point of view is of obvious importance, but good ethnographic films may be made from countless different points of view, and there is no reasonable way to arrange points of view on an attribute dimension grid, even one as loosely calibrated as this.

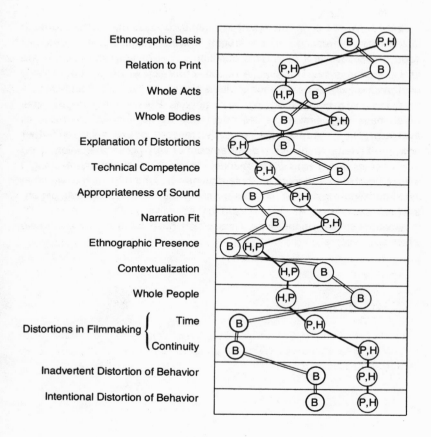

Diagram 3. The attribute dimension grid, constructed from the attribute dimensions in diagram 2. The attributes are listed in decreasing order of criticalness, and the more ethnographic values are to the right. Profiles of ethnographicness have been plotted on the grid for three films, *Dead Birds* (B), *Dani Sweet Potatoes* (P), and *Dani Houses* (H).

And I have not even attempted to quantify or systematize an approach to the most interesting and challenging critical evaluations: namely, how good or effective is a film? This question is not entirely unrelated to the attribute dimensions, however. A documentary film which got consistently unethnographic ratings on each attribute dimension would probably not be considered very highly in any sense by anyone. But two ethnographic films which have very similar profiles could well evoke very different overall evaluations from viewers. I am not really prepared to take this much further now, for it seems to involve a great amount of very personal opinion, even when ostensibly dealing with "science." It may be that with more thought we will be able to add more attribute dimensions. Or it may be that we have systematized things about as far as we can. At any rate, the attribute dimension grid provides a firm and reasonably objective platform from which to think about those ethnographic films which have been made and those which are to come.

Ethnographic Basis	
Relation to Print	
Whole Acts	
Whole Bodies	
Explanation of Distortions	
Technical Competence	
Appropriateness of Sound	
Narration Fit	
Ethnographic Presence	
Contextualization	
Whole People	
Distortions in Filmmaking { Time	
{ Continuity	
Inadvertent Distortion of Behavior	
Intentional Distortion of Behavior	

Diagram 4. The attribute dimension grid.

Chapter 4

Making Ethnographic Film

This book is more about the ethnographicness of films than about films in general. Likewise, this chapter contains thoughts about how to make films more ethnographic, and it does not attempt to cover all aspects of filmmaking. The basic technology of filmmaking is the same for all films, however ethnographic they attempt to be. This technology can be learned in cinematography classes, and some people can do much learning on their own with the help of excellent recent books on filmmaking (e.g., Pincus 1969; Lipton 1972).

The Ethics of Ethnographic Filmmaking

The making of an ethnographic film raises extraordinarily complex ethical questions. Especially since the mid-1960s, anthropologists in the United States have been attempting to spell out in some detail their ethical responsibilities. This is difficult enough for ordinary ethnographic research; for ethnographic filmmaking, it is almost impossible. It is worthwhile to quote at some length from the Principles of Professional Responsibility adopted by the Council of the American Anthropological Association, May 1971:

Preamble:

Anthropologists work in many parts of the world in close personal association with the peoples and situations they study. Their professional situation is, therefore, uniquely varied and complex. They are involved with their discipline, their colleagues, their students, their sponsors, their subjects, their own and host governments, the particular individuals and groups with whom they do their field work, other populations and interest groups in the nations within which they work and the study of processes and issues affecting general human welfare. In a field of such complex involvements, misunderstandings, conflicts and the necessity to make choices among conflicting values are bound to arise and to generate ethical dilemmas. It is a prime responsibility of anthropologists to anticipate these and to plan to resolve them in such a way as to do damage neither to those whom they study nor, in so far as possible, to their scholarly community. Where these conditions cannot be met, the anthropologist would be well-advised not to pursue the particular piece of research.

The following principles are deemed fundamental to the anthropologist's responsible, ethical pursuit of his profession.

1. *Relations with those studied:*

In research, an anthropologist's paramount responsibility is to those he studies. When there is a conflict of interest, these individuals must come first. The anthropologist must do everything within his power to protect their physical, social and psychological welfare and to honor their dignity and privacy.

   a. Where research involves the acquisition of material and information transferred on the assumption of trust between persons, it is axiomatic that the rights, interests, and sensitivities of those studied must be safeguarded.

   b. The aims of the investigation should be communicated as well as possible to the informant.

   c. Informants have a right to remain anonymous. This right should be respected both where it has been promised explicitly and where no clear understanding to the contrary has been reached. These strictures apply to the collection of data by means of cameras, tape recorders, and other data-gathering devices, as well as to data collected in face-to-face interviews or in participant observation. Those being studied should understand the capacities of such devices; they should be free to reject them if they wish; and if they accept them, the results obtained should be consonant with the informant's right to welfare, dignity and privacy.

   d. There should be no exploitation of individual informants for personal gain. Fair return should be given them for all services.

   e. There is an obligation to reflect on the foreseeable repercussions of research and publication on the general population being studied.

   f. The anticipated consequences of research should be communicated as fully as possible to the individuals and groups likely to be affected.

   g. In accordance with the Association's general position on clandestine and secret research, no reports should be provided to sponsors that are not also available to the general public and where practicable, to the population studied.

h. Every effort should be exerted to cooperate with members of the host society in the planning and execution of research projects.

i. All of the above points should be acted upon in full recognition of the social and cultural pluralism of host societies and the consequent plurality of values, interests and demands in those societies. This diversity complicates choice-making in research, but ignoring it leads to irresponsible decisions. (American Anthropological Association 1973:1)

These demands seem impossibly stringent. But they are all based on a single underlying imperative: we have a responsibility to do nothing which will harm the people we study and film. The great problem, of course, is to anticipate the potential damage which a film might do to the people's "physical, social and psychological welfare" as well as to "their dignity and privacy." The ethnographic filmmaker, as well as the ethnographer, must be aware of the considerable responsibility which accompanies the license to study and to film.

The conscientious ethnographic filmmaker will avoid the more obviously unethical practices. But it really is not possible for people to give fully informed permission for their images to be used in a film. When I was filming the Dani in West Irian in 1963, I made no attempt to explain what films were all about. I simply did not think that it could be done in any meaningful way. In fact, Frederick Wiseman's experiences in filming U.S. institutions turned up quite remarkable evidence that even people in the United States, who are ostensibly highly sophisticated about movies and television, cannot make informed decisions of the sort demanded by the ethics statement.

Wiseman described his procedure in an interview in *Filmmakers Newsletter*: "If anyone objects either before, during, or immediately after a sequence is shot, I don't use it; but I don't give anyone the right of review thereafter" (Halberstadt 1974:21).

But the problem is that at the moment of shooting no one can really know how the footage will turn out, or how he or she will appear. And the subject certainly cannot anticipate what will be preserved, omitted, or juxtaposed during the editing. And also, it turns out that even when people see themselves in a finished film, they cannot anticipate how that film will affect others. It is especially true with the subjects of ethnographic films, who for the most part have never been in a film before.

This was illustrated by the controversy which arose around Wiseman's 1974 television film, "Primate," which was about the Yerkes Primate Research Center. In a letter to the editor of the *New York Times* (December 15, 1974), Dr. Geoffrey H. Bourne, director of the center, objected to the Wiseman film on the grounds that it "not just distorts the truth but actually inverts it so that the scenes are telling lies." The next week (December 22, 1974), Wiseman replied in defense that no one had objected during the filming, and that Bourne apparently had had no objections to the finished film until he saw the reviews.

The dilemma is evident. If a filmmaker acknowledges that he has an obligation to obtain permission, or releases, from the people in the film, then how can he arbitrarily declare that the obligation is fulfilled at the time of shooting, and thereafter the subjects have no more rights? On the other hand, if the subjects exercised rights of review throughout, then very few films would ever be finished. This is a very complex ethical as well as legal question, and the American Anthropological Association statement on ethics is of little help. As long as the subjects of ethnographic films were ten thousand miles away from the audiences, there seemed to be little real problem. But now that ethnographers are making films in the United States, and people in New Guinea are using films themselves, the situation has changed. I shall not pretend to offer any answers, but I must emphasize that filmmakers should keep these considerations in mind. Ethnography and filmmaking cannot guarantee always to produce studies which are thoroughly pleasing to all involved, but they should at least not be vulnerable to charges of falsification of a situation.

The Finances of Ethnographic Filmmaking

It is worth emphasizing at the outset that filmmaking is much more than shooting footage. It takes an immense amount of time, money, and equipment to actually complete a film. Shooting the footage is only the first, easiest, least expensive, and, for most people, the most satisfying step. Every neighborhood camera store can sell a camera, tripod, light meter, and film, and then for additional money will process the film. It is like life: it is absurdly easy to get married, or create a baby; but, after this first easy step, the next stages are incredibly difficult. So in film, there is a false sense of achievement in having actually shot footage. Then comes the letdown, when the long dreary process of editing looms ahead. An appalling number of anthropologists return from the field with footage which they have shot but with little idea why they shot it, and less idea of what to do with it. Sometimes they edit out the worst scenes and the blank leader and show the rest to a class or two. But gradually it is forgotten and sits on a bookshelf collecting dust.

One 100-ft. roll of 16-mm. color film runs for a little less than three minutes. It has an apparent price tag of, say, $8. But this is camera-shop seduction. Once the roll is shot, it costs another $5 to have it developed. And if it is worth using, a work-print copy must be made to use in the first step of editing, so as to protect the original—another $5. Then, even if it is very good, as much as one-half of the roll will wind up in the finished film (this is a 2:1 shooting ratio, and extraordinarily optimistic; in fact, 5:1 or 10:1 is more likely). Let us suppose that one minute of that roll ends up in the finished film. If it is a twenty-minute film, we can figure 1/20 of the cost of the final processing to get to a distribution print, or somewhere around $50. So the original $8 purchase price has hidden costs in the neighborhood of $50 to $75 if anything is to come of the film. And this is not counting time and labor. Realistically, one to four hours in the field may be taken up with shooting three minutes of film. Several more hours of editing will be devoted to that one reel. Multiply this by ten reels or fifty reels or whatever an anthropologist has taken into the field. Or, figure that the film alone for a twenty-minute film represents a cash investment of at least a thousand dollars (not even counting the camera, etc.), plus hundreds of hours of labor, plus access to expensive editing equipment.

Let me give another rough estimate of expenses. In a class on ethnographic film which I taught at Stanford University in 1974, ten students made proposals for ethnographic films, complete with budgets. The films were to be between twenty and sixty minutes long. Their estimated expenses ranged from $2,000 to $41,000, with an average of $18,000. All this is in the unreadable fine print when an anthropologist trustingly buys camera and film and sets out for the field. Small wonder that the film so often ends up untouched in cardboard boxes.

Obviously, most ethnographic filmmakers need money from somewhere. In some countries a certain amount of ethnographic filmmaking takes place under the auspices of a permanent government-supported institution like the National Film Board in Canada, or the Institute for Aboriginal Studies in Australia. Outright commercial sponsorship will probably never be a major factor in ethnographic film production. Some films, like some books, which are made according to scientific standards, may also be commercially successful, but this is a happy coincidence, and not predictable enough to attract much capital. Robert Flaherty tried it, but the financial results of his various films would probably not encourage anyone to repeat it.

In the United States, at any rate, foundation grants seem to be the most reasonable way to finance ethnographic films. In addition to the foundations which support other anthropological research, there are those like the National Endowment for the Arts and the National Endowment for the Humanities. Robert Mugge has described these latter sources in a pair of recent articles which should be of interest to ethnographic filmmakers (1974).

There is no particular secret about getting grants. Ethnographic film proposals should be presented in the same way in which other ethnographic research is presented. Presumably funds will be granted to a film proposal which is well thought out and which promises to result in a film which is truly ethnographic. Looking back at the 1960s from the mid-1970s, it seems to have been a time when grant money was so plentiful that all proposals were funded. To a great extent this is a nostalgic myth. But there is no question that money for anthropology is tighter than it has been. General proposals, framed merely in terms of disappearing cultures which need to be filmed by talented filmmakers, probably will have as little chance of success as a comparably phrased proposal for nonfilm research. When funds are scarce, those resources available for ethnography will properly go to those projects which have the greatest ethnographic importance and the best chance to produce high-level ethnographic results.

All this has been addressed to anthropologists in the interests of sobering reality. Any cinematographer or comprehensive camera store could provide the same information on costs, if sought out and asked. But a more important question, and one with a less obvious answer, is how can one proceed to make a film more ethnographic? The preceding chapter has analyzed, point by point, the attributes which make films ethnographic. If taken to heart and used sensibly, not as automatic cookbook directives, these attributes can point the way. But here a few general summary principles can be drawn up.

An Ethnographic Film Must Be Based on Ethnographic Understanding

This principle is so obvious and fundamental that it is tautological. And yet it is resisted explicitly or implicitly by most cinematographers involved in ethnographic film. I would go further and say that when films are made on subjects of ethnographic concern, the use of ethnographic understandings not only makes films more ethnographic, but also better films aesthetically. One of the strongest examples is *The Nuer*. It could have been immensely improved as a film if the filmmakers had understood more of what was happening, and it would not have had to lose any of its aesthetic qualities.

If a film is to be informed by ethnographic understanding, it is virtually essential that a knowledgeable ethnographer be intimately involved *as ethnographer* in each step of the filmmaking process. It is not enough merely to have a token ethnographer present, perhaps holding a microphone, as was apparently the case with many ethnographic film projects.

The ideal arrangement is for the ethnographer to do the field work first, complete the analysis and writing, and then return to the scene with a filmmaker to shoot a film which has been carefully thought out on the basis of the written work. This course was followed in making *The Feast* and *Kypseli*. After Chagnon had spent two years studying the Yanomamö of southern Venezuela and had written his booklet, he returned with Timothy Asch to film chapter four as *The Feast*; after Susannah Hoffman had spent a year studying the Greek village of Kypseli and had completed her Ph.D. dissertation on sex roles in the village, she returned with Paul Aratow and Richard Cowan to film her dissertation. My own films, *Dani Sweet Potatoes* and *Dani Houses*, were shot on my second trip to the Dani, after I had spent nearly two years studying Dani horticulture and construction. The filmic quality of all these films varies considerably, but they are more ethnographic than any films made only by competent cinematographers could possibly be.

For various reasons, the ethnography and the cinematography may be done concurrently. This is true, for example, of the Bateson and Mead Balinese films, of *Dead Birds*, and of *The Turtle People*. This can be fairly effective and is relatively economical. But in most ethnographic studies, the full implications of the study are not realized until the end of the study, or even until the analysis is complete, long after leaving the field. The study can be described quite satisfactorily in sentences forged then. But no new footage can be shot, and a partial salvage job is often necessary—patching over inadequate footage with an informed but ex post facto narration.

The worst cases are the real salvage jobs, where some well-intentioned but ethnographically naïve person shoots footage and then brings cans of film to an anthropologist or editor to ask what can be done. Except in the rarest of cases the footage is a total loss.

The saddest cases are anthropologists who have shot film of situations which they knew very well, but without thinking in filmic terms, and usually with cameras which they had bought in a tax-free shop enroute to the field and have had no experience in using—indeed, haven't even had time to test for mechanical failure.

In short, it is not enough that an ethnographer (or an ethnography) be available. The ethnographic film must emerge from the ethnographic understanding. But not all ethnographic insights are equally filmic.

Ethnographic Film Must Exploit the Visual Potential of Film

A picture is worth 10,000 words. But not any picture, and not any words. The major conceptual step from ethnography to film is to decide what aspects of the ethnography can be described more effectively in film, or for which aspects the verbal description of the ethnography can best be supplemented by film.

The answer is different in each case. As a nice exercise in this sort of thinking, one can take any important article or monograph in the anthropological literature and work out a film which would best enhance these specific written words. One can conjure with all the possibilities of film to show holistic interrelationships of people and landscapes; the infinite nuances of human interaction; styles of expression and movement; ambience, tempo, and feeling of group events, and processes from beginning to end. One can use film of naturally occurring events, acted events, or animation.

Whole Bodies and Whole People in Whole Acts

This is a useful ethnographic dictum for an ethnographic filmmaker. Close-up shots of faces should be used very sparingly, for entire bodies of people at work or play or rest are more revealing and interesting than body fragments. Events should be shown from beginning to end. In *Dani Houses*, I was concerned with showing the entire sequence of house construction. Now, thinking about that film in retrospect, I wish that I had gone on to show how the houses were used. I did show a whole process, and there is a real sense of closure with the last shot of the newly finished house in the late afternoon sun. It is a satisfactory account of a whole act. But I now think it would have been much stronger if I had defined the subject as construction *and* use of Dani houses.

Division of Labor

Should one person be both filmmaker and anthropologist? Or should there be a filmmaker in addition to the anthropologist? This is a strongly debated question, and it is usually resolved on the grounds of available financing, or other extrinsic considerations. This may be the best way to answer the question, rather than taking a definitive stand on theoretical grounds. I do think that it is unreasonable for one person to expect to be able to fulfill the duties of both ethnographer and filmmaker in the field, and it is even harder to do both tasks in the postfield period. In most cases where one person has tried to do both, the ethnography or the film has suffered, or the completion of one or both has been inordinately delayed. The success of teams in making the Netsilik Eskimo films, *Dead Birds*, *The Feast*, *Kypseli*, and *Desert People*, to name just a few, supports the argument that one person should be the filmmaker, another the ethnographer. But it is also essential that each person should understand and respect the métier of the other. This may be the most difficult obstacle to overcome. Jean Rouch (1974) argues strongly against a team on the grounds that the extra people are simply too disruptive of the situation. He favors a single anthropologist/cameraman assisted by a local person trained as a sound man.

The Meaning of Real Collaboration

The *Hadza* is a good example of a film made by a skilled filmmaker and a very knowledgeable anthropologist, but it shows a lack of real collaborative thought. The Hadza are a tribe of hunters and gatherers in Tanzania who, like many such groups, have considerable leisure time. The main activity of the men seems to be gambling. The film includes a long sequence of gambling activity, and the narration explains the rules of the game and the general cultural context of gambling for the Hadza. But the visuals are general shots, and the narration might as well have been written before the footage was shot. They are of the same subject, but are not successfully coordinated.

The filmmakers should have phrased their problem in terms like this: What is especially visual about this activity, and how can it best be shown on film? They do show the group of men sitting around the gambling spot, and one man throwing disks against a tree. So far so good. It is a good setting shot, showing whole people. But gambling is surely entertainment and interaction, with winners and losers, involving some emotional investment, some strategies; yet none of this was captured in the visuals. The *Hadza* has achieved a major degree of ethnographicness, not only in the informed narration but also in the way in which the visuals do cover the ethnographically important aspects of Hadza life. But yet it falls short of maximal ethnographic use of film. It was good to say "gambling is important so we need a gambling scene." But the next, most creative step was not taken, where the question is "what is ethnographically important and visually accessible?"

We are talking about what might be called an inductive approach: starting with an understanding of the facts and then shooting for them. Certainly the *Hadza* is a far cry from the other approach, which involves shooting for interesting scenes and actions and then putting together some sort of statement.

An Ethnographic Film Cannot Stand by Itself

This axiom may be an affront to a traditional filmmaker, but it is obvious to the anthropologist who has seen and thought about an ethnographic film. An ethnographic film must arise from an ethnographic understanding of a culture, and it can present much at which the words of a written ethnography can only hint. On the other hand, no film can communicate all the information which we can legitimately ask of ethnography. In particular we need to know the circumstances of the ethnographic research and the filmmaking and the cultural context of the behavior, much of which involves generalizations of fact and abstract concepts. These are essentially verbal, not visual. Some sense of them may be printed in titles or read as narration, but only at the risk of detracting from the visual power of the film.

In short, while film can play an important role in ethnographic description, it cannot satisfy all ethnography's needs. An ethnographic film must be supplemented by written material. Just as the making of an ethnographic film must be one part of an ethnographic research enterprise, so the results must include both film and printed material.

Film versus Videotape

As videotape becomes cheaper, more portable and versatile, and less vulnerable to malfunction, it will begin to be used for ethnographic films. Its great advantages over film are its portability, the low cost of the tape, the fact that it records and can immediately play back synchronous sound, and its technical abilities to record in dim light and make half-hour or longer takes with the basic equipment. The major disadvantages of videotape are the relatively coarse resolution of its images and the danger that the sensitive electronic equipment will irreparably break down in an isolated field situation.

But the ease of recording synchronous sound sequences of behavioral events makes videotape an exceptionally promising ethnographic tool. There is also a danger in this very ease of shooting long tape sequences: many people get carried away with videotape and produce long records made for the joy of shooting, with no idea of how they are to be used.

Ethnographic Films from Research Footage

The use of film and videotape records as primary data for anthropological research has only begun. For example, much research on what is loosely called nonverbal behavior requires a microlevel of analysis which can only be done by repeated frame-by-frame viewing. The film itself is then the data and should be published as part of the technical report. However, there are many technical problems which have not yet been overcome in "publishing" film with a journal article.

Ray Birdwhistell made a study of *Microcultural Incidents in Ten Zoos*, and his only report to date is a film made of a lecture presented in 1968 under that title. The film incorporates the original footage, slowed down and repeated where necessary to point out the more subtle actions. Another film, *Invisible Walls*, by Richard Cowan and Lucy Turner, shows the results of a study of proxemics, or personal space. And *Maring in Motion*, made by Marek Jablonko, is a compilation of research footage used by Alison Jablonko in her choreometric study of New Guinea Maring motion. Jablonko's dissertation is available through Xerox University Microfilms (Ann Arbor, Michigan), but neither Birdwhistell nor Cowan and Turner have published the details of their studies. As this kind of research increases, some way must be found to publish the results of both film and articles.

Preservation of the Film Record

Footage shot by anthropologists, especially of rapidly changing tribal cultures, represents an invaluable record and source of data which must be preserved for future generations of the subjects themselves and for scientists who will be engaged in research as yet unimagined. Whatever the possibility of this footage as ethnographic film today, it should be annotated and preserved. Film which is lost is irreplaceable. One of the horror stories of anthropology tells of the footage taken by A. L. Kroeber of Ishi, the last "wild" California Indian, in 1914. According to the story, the footage was stored near a heating pipe in the University of California museum and simply baked out of existence. Footage should be stored in a vault with temperature and humidity controls.

But unless the footage is annotated, it is nearly as good as lost. E. Richard Sorenson, who worked with Carleton Gajdusek in the National Institute of Mental Health film archive, in Bethesda, Maryland, has spent considerable time in setting up the National Anthropological Film Center at the Smithsonian Institution (see Sorenson 1967 and 1974). This archive will allow anthropologists and others to deposit their film, with annotations, in a secure place where others would have access to it.

Chapter 5

The Use of Ethnographic Films in Teaching

Most instructors who use ethnographic films at all woefully underuse them. At worst, ethnographic films serve as baby-sitting devices to fill a few sessions while the instructor is out of town or otherwise disinclined to give a lecture. For the students, film sessions usually result in pleasant experiences in dark rooms, but little more. Even when instructors wish to make good use of films, they rarely have anywhere to turn. The books which they use they have read in advance and can set into perspective, but not so with films. Most film rental contracts are for one showing only, and, even if the film is locally owned, the effort of setting up extra screenings overwhelms most teachers. So films are shown with minimal knowledge or preparation and only seen once—unlike a book, which can be read carefully, and parts reread, more or less at leisure. Birdwhistell, in his excellent discussion of this whole problem, recommends a minimum of two preview screenings for each film (1963). But this is hardly ever done, even by the most conscientious instructors. I am not sure whether to be discouraged thoroughly that films are used in such a casual way or to be heartened that, despite so many problems, films are so widely used.

Of course, most of us encounter films almost exclusively in the context of movie entertainment or, in the form of television commercials, as sales propaganda. As a result, we are trained so thoroughly in one mode of seeing that this poses a major obstacle to the use of film in teaching, where the entertainment and propaganda values are less important than the purely informational value. It is much easier for a student to gain intellectual content and stimulation from a book than from a film. And yet, that intellectual content and stimulation are just what we hope ethnographic films can somehow provide.

One purpose of this book is to indicate how to make films which are more ethnographic. And as films become more ethnographic, they will be more usable for teaching ethnography (also, see Asch 1974).

Films and Background Reading

In 1966 I assembled the first edition of the catalogue *Films for Anthropological Teaching*. This first edition listed some 90 films. By the fifth edition in

1972, there were over 450 titles. Much of this increase represents ethnographic films completed between 1966 and 1972. The catalogue lists film titles, credits, distributors, descriptions, and, most important, a bibliography of related printed materials.

The first requirement for using an ethnographic film in teaching is that the instructor know the film well enough to incorporate it into the course. The instructor should be able to read material about the cultural events depicted in the film and should have seen the film and be able to prepare the class for it. Just as one usually prepares students to read a monograph by alerting them to certain key problems, so can one prepare students to view a film. With printed material, students can always return to it to read for more understanding. This is rarely done with films, although the advantages are strong. Ideally there would be a preparatory lecture, then a first screening, followed by discussion, and then a second screening followed by what would certainly be a much deeper discussion. As long as ethnographic films are merely time-wasting entertainments, real discussions do not take place, and second screenings would be pointless. But when an ethnographic film can be understood, it can be exploited in this way. And, of course, unless it is exploited in this way, it cannot be understood. However, this is not really an unbreakable vicious circle. The key to understanding an ethnographic film, or gaining information from it, is not just repeated viewings but the availability of written materials which can fill in what the film leaves ambiguous.

The catalogue *Films for Anthropological Teaching* lists as much as possible of the literature related to each film which will allow classes to understand the film. Unfortunately, few films have anything approaching useful related literature. There are many problems.

For example, *Grass* shows the dramatic semiannual migration of the Bakhtiari herdsmen of Persia. The filmmaker's popular account of their adventure (Cooper 1925) is long since out of print, and I know of no ethnographic study of the Bakhtiari which could answer the questions which the film raises. The closest is Fredrik Barth's work on similar groups several hundred miles to the south of the Bakhtiari (1961). Another sort of problem is availability: Bateson and Mead wrote an excellent book, *Balinese Character* (1942), which nicely complements their Balinese films, but the book is scarce and expensive, and so cannot be used conveniently for classes.

The Nuer was filmed on the culture which E. E. Evans-Pritchard had studied thirty years earlier, and his books and articles are easily available. In fact, his monograph, *The Nuer* (1940), is widely used in paperback edition in classes. But the film is so nonethnographic that the more an instructor knows about the culture, the less likely he is to be willing to use the film. I would argue strongly that while the film has many ethnographic short-comings, it can be used to good advantage. It does capture some of the ambience of a Nuer cattle camp and is an exquisitely beautiful film. It can be seen by students before they read the monograph. One problem with asking students to read technical monographs in classes is that, when the culture is too exotic, it is difficult for students to make much sense of the monograph. Seeing *The Nuer* film gives them a kind of holistic impression-istic sense for the Nuer, and so they have some cognitive landscape, some place to anchor what they read. I would think that the eighty-three minutes spent seeing the film would be worth far more than an extra eighty-three minutes rereading the monograph, in terms of understanding even abstract principles of lineage organization.

On the other hand, *Tidikawa and Friends*, an equally beautiful impres-sionistic film made in New Guinea, is less useful in this way. It was made about a people for whom there is no written ethnographic data; and to use it as background for reading about a different New Guinea culture could be misleading. (I suppose, in fact, that *Dead Birds* has this drawback—it is about the Dani of West New Guinea, and most of the ethnographic litera-ture on the New Guinea Highlands is about cultures which lie hundreds of miles to the east of the Dani, and which are somewhat similar but in impor-tant ways very different. It is quite possible that after a person has seen *Dead Birds* he will read "Dani" into all the rest of New Guinea Highland literature.)

The Dani research represents the most comprehensive coverage to date. The same events shown in Gardner's film *Dead Birds* and my two short films, *Dani Sweet Potatoes* and *Dani Houses*, are described and analyzed in several books and articles by the various members of the Harvard Pea-body Expedition (see Matthiessen 1962; Broekhuijse 1967; Gardner and Heider 1969; K. G. Heider 1969, 1972a). The most important of these for teaching purposes is a 75-page pamphlet (or module) called *The Dani of West Irian: An Ethnographic Companion to the Film "Dead Birds"* (Heider 1972b). This ethnographic companion is specifically designed to be used by instructors and assigned to students in connection with the film. It in-cludes a 26-page ethnographic sketch of the Dani, more or less a condensa-tion of my 330-page ethnography on the Dani, but with special reference to events shown in the film; an essay by Robert Gardner in which he discusses why and how he made the film; and a shot-by-shot analysis of the 663 shots in the film, printed in double column alongside the narration of the film.

The purpose of the ethnographic companion is to increase the accessibility of the information of the film. It was really made as an afterthought, when it became clear that something was needed to bridge the gap between our technical writings about the Dani and the film. But now we can expect more and more ethnographic films to be made concurrently with this sort of written accompaniment.

Technology

Petty technical problems can overwhelm the best of films. Incompetent or just inexperienced projectionists, sound systems with miniscule, tinny-toned, ill-placed speakers, and old, damaged screens, are the most common occurrences. The solutions are obvious, but they do cost money, and such funds are among the most begrudged in both schools and colleges.

Strategies

The most common strategy in using an ethnographic film in teaching is to screen the film once, perhaps preceded by some introduction and followed by some discussion. An extremely simple but effective variation is to show the film twice. Because ethnographic films are of such totally unfamiliar subjects, the first viewing tends to inundate audiences with indigestible impressions. The real appreciation and absorption of filmic data increase tremendously with a second viewing. (I am tempted to say "increase immeasurably," but the increase is probably measurable and could be the subject of a useful study in itself.)

Another very effective use of ethnographic films in teaching is to show a film, or part of a film, without sound, and to ask the students to study it as raw data. James Deetz, the archaeologist, first suggested this to me, and I have subsequently tried it, using a twenty-minute section from *Dead Birds* (the first part of the second reel). First the students see that twenty minutes, without narration, and write down what they think was happening. Then they see the entire film from the beginning, with narration, and once again write what was happening, in the key twenty minutes, paying special attention to how and why they might have been wrong in their first interpretations of the action.

This strategy is quite effective in heightening students' appreciation of film as data. They not only have studied that film with extraordinary concentration, but they have also taken an important step toward seeing film in general through more sensitive eyes.

Appendix

A Brief Descriptive Catalogue of Films

Although this book does not attempt to make a full description or critique of any one film, there are references to more than fifty films scattered throughout it. The following is a list of most of those films, with description and bibliography, more or less freely adapted from the catalogue *Films for Anthropological Teaching*, fifth edition (Heider 1972c). The catalogue itself lists some 450 titles and is obtainable from the American Anthropological Association, 1703 New Hampshire Avenue NW, Washington, D.C. 20009. There are many chances for error in a catalogue such as this. Credits are not standardized, and it is often difficult to tell from titles like "filmmaker," "director," "anthropologist," and "producer" just what a person's role in the filmmaking was. Distributors change and prices rise constantly. I have listed some distributors, trying in each case to give at least the primary distributor (the source for purchasing prints), together with some rental sources. I have not even attempted to give sale and rental prices.

It is also worth mentioning here the three comprehensive UNESCO catalogues:

1967. *Premier catalogue sélectif international de films ethnographiques sur l'Afrique noire.*

1970. *Premier catalogue sélectif international de films ethnographiques sur la région du Pacifique.*

1970. *Catalogue de films d'intérêt archaeologique, ethnographique ou historique.*

These are published by UNESCO, Place de Fontenoy, 75 Paris-7e, France, and may be obtained from UniPub, Inc., P.O. Box 433, New York, New York 10022.

Distributors

B&C   B&C Films, 10451 Selkirk Lane, Los Angeles, California 90024.

C5   Cinema Five, 595 Madison Avenue, New York, New York 10022.

CHF   Churchill Films, 662 N. Robertson Boulevard, Los Angeles, California 90069.

Cont/McG-H   McGraw-Hill Contemporary Films, Inc., Princeton Road, Hightstown, New Jersey 08520.

828 Custer Avenue, Evanston, Illinois 60202.

1714 Stockton Street, San Francisco, California 94133.

DER	Documentary Educational Resources, 24 Dane Street, Somerville, Massachusetts 02143.
HR&W	Holt, Rinehart & Winston, Inc. Media Department, 383 Madison Avenue, New York, New York 10017.
IFB	International Film Bureau, Inc., 332 S. Michigan Avenue, Chicago, Illinois 60604.
IU	Indiana University, Audio-Visual Center, Bloomington, Indiana 47401.
MOMA	Museum of Modern Art, 11 W. 53rd Street, New York, New York 10019.
NYU	New York University Film Library, 26 Washington Place, New York, New York 10003.
Phoenix	Phoenix Films, 470 Park Avenue So., New York, New York 10016.
PSU	Pennsylvania State University Audio-Visual Services, University Park, Pennsylvania 16802.
RBMU	Regions Beyond Missionary Union, 8102 Elberon Avenue, Philadelphia, Pennsylvania 19111.
SPF	Special Purpose Films, 26740 Latigo Shore Drive, Malibu, California 90265.
Sumai	The Sumai Film Company, Box 26481, Los Angeles, California 90026.
UCEMC	University of California Extension Media Center, 2223 Fulton Street, Berkeley, California 94720.
UEVA	Universal Education and Visual Arts, Inc., 221 Park Avenue South, New York, New York 10003.
USNAC	United States National Audiovisual Center, Washington, D.C. 20409.
Zia	Zia Cine, P.O. Box 493, Santa Fe, New Mexico 87501.

"An American Family" (1973). A twelve-part series produced for WNET (television) by Craig Gilbert. Not currently in distribution.

A dramatic, controversial documentary about a middle-class white family living in Santa Barbara, California. Unique for its length, its intimacy, and its nonexoticness (for the U.S. television audience). A major subject of conversation among intellectuals in the United States during mid-1973. The controversies focused on the filmmaking process and on the nature of the culture depicted. Most viewers had a much better basis for making judgments than they do for most "ethnographic" films.

Bibliography.

Goulart, Ron. 1973. *An American family.* New York: Warner Paperback Library.

Loud, Pat, with Nora Johnson. 1974. *Pat Loud: A woman's story.* New York: Coward, McCann & Geoghegan.

Raymond, Alan and Susan. 1973. Filming an American family. *Filmmakers newsletter* 6.5:19–21.

The American Indian Series (1961–1965). Includes *Acorns: Staple Food of California Indians; Basketry of the Pomo* (three films); *Beautiful Tree— Chishkale; Buckeyes: Food of California Indians; Calumet, Pipe of Peace; Dream Dances of the Kashia Pomo; Game of Staves; Kashia Men's Dances; Obsidian Point-Making; Pine Nuts; Pomo Shaman; Sinew-Backed Bow; Sucking Doctor; Totem Pole; Wooden Box: Made by Steaming and Bending.*

Made under the anthropological direction of Samuel A. Barrett of the Department of Anthropology, University of California at Berkeley. The project was begun during the 1950s and the films released during the early 1960s. Produced by University of California Extension Media Center. Filmmakers involved included Clyde Smith, William Heick, Ernest Rose, Al Fiering, Cameron Macauley, Robert Wharton, and David Perri. Distributed by UCEMC.

Most of these films show California Indians, especially Kashia Pomo. The technology films range from fairly narrow reconstructions to broadly conceived holistic accounts (e.g., *Beautiful Tree—Chishkale*). There are four Pomo ritual films. Barrett died before the completion of this project, and extensive ethnographic documentation is not available.

The Anasternaria (1969). 17 min. Rental by UCEMC.

Follows the spectacular Christian/pagan spring ritual of Macedonian

Greeks. Includes ecstatic trance states and walking on hot coals. The narration gives a heavily analytic (Jungian) interpretation of events.

Appeals to Santiago (ca. 1967). 28 min. Made by Arnold Baskin in collaboration with Carter Wilson, Duane Metzger, and Robert Ravicz. Distributed by Cont/McG-H.

Follows the "cargo" ritual of the Chiapas (Mexico) Maya, in which different men assume the responsibility of caring for saints' images over the course of a year. Describes the ritual from the Mayan point of view (in contrast to Cancian's economic explanation).

Bibliography.
Cancian, Frank. 1965. *Economics and prestige in a Maya community.* Stanford: Stanford University Press.

An Argument about a Marriage (1968?). 18 min. One of the new films made from John Marshall's footage shot in the 1950s. Distributed by DER.

A dense film which tries to follow an intricate conflict between two groups of Kalahari Bushmen. The first part of the film uses English narration over stills to explain the argument and its historical and cultural context; then the film follows the argument as it developed, using only postsynchronized Bushman voices with English subtitles.

Bibliography. See bibliography for *The Hunters*, below.
Reichlin, Seth, and John Marshall. 1974. *An argument about a marriage: The study guide.* Somerville, Mass.: Documentary Educational Resources.

Baboons of Gombe (1974). A film made for ABC television by Hugo van Lawick. Not in distribution yet.

Focuses on the Beach Troop of baboons on the banks of Lake Tanganyika, at the Gombe Stream Reserve, where Jane Goodall has been studying chimpanzees since 1960. An important sequence shows a newcomer maneuvering for leadership in the troop.

Bitter Melons (1968?). 30 min. One of the new films made from John Marshall's footage shot in 1955 in the Kalahari Desert—perhaps the earliest synchronous sound shot in the field. Edited by Frank Galvin. Distributed by DER. Rental by UCEMC.

Focuses on a Kalahari Bushman who composes songs and melodies for the one string bow. The different pieces he plays cover a wide range of Bushman concerns. By the device of starting each sequence with the music in synchronized sound and then cutting to visuals which illustrate his themes, the film covers a wide range of topics in Bushman culture.

Bibliography. See the bibliography for *The Hunters*, below.

Reichlin, Seth. 1974. *Bitter melons: A study guide*. Somerville, Mass.: Documentary Educational Resources.

Childhood Rivalry in Bali and New Guinea (1952). 17 min. Made by Gregory Bateson and Margaret Mead in 1936–1938. Distributed by NYU. Rental by UCEMC and others.

The first filmic attempt to be comparative explicitly. It shows comparable scenes from two different cultures: Bali and the Iatmul of the Sepik River in New Guinea. Uses some naturally occurring similar situations, e.g., ear piercing, and also "experimental," or created, situations, such as giving a doll to a child to provoke rivalry reactions.

Bibliography. See bibliography for *Trance and Dance in Bali*.

Chronicle of a Summer (1961). Ca. 90 min. Made by Jean Rouch and Edgar Morin. Distributed by Cont/McG-H.

The first synchronous sound, *cinéma vérité* film about the attempts of an anthropologist (Jean Rouch) and a sociologist (Edgar Morin) to discover what Parisians were thinking in the summer of 1960. It is mainly talk, with practically no "action." Unsurpassed for self-conscious honesty in showing Rouch and Morin in the film asking questions, influencing events; native feedback when the first version is shown to the people and they respond; and final scenes where Rouch and Morin discuss their achievement.

Bibliography.

Freyer, Ellen. 1971. Chronicle of a summer—ten years after. In *The documentary tradition*, edited by Lewis Jacobs, pp. 437–443. New York: Hopkinson & Blake.

Levin, G. Roy. 1971. Jean Rouch. In *Documentary explorations*, edited by G. Roy Levin, pp. 131–145. Garden City, New York: Doubleday.

The Cows of Dolo Ken Paye: Resolving Conflict among the Kpelle (1970). 32 min. Made by Marvin Silverman in collaboration with the anthropologist James L. Gibbs, Jr. Distributed by HR&W.

Gibbs's description (from K. G. Heider 1972c:18–19):

The wounding of a crop-eating cow by a Kpelle farmer starts a dispute which is followed to its conclusion in a hot-knife trial by ordeal. Photographed in Fokwelle, Liberia, in 1968, the film shows the conflict as it actually unfolded. Events filmed before the wounding of a cow indicate that the outburst was not random, but rooted in the ways in which cattle are used and in the complex relationships of the prosperous, cattle-owning chiefs and the ordinary farmers who are their constituents. Flashbacks of actual events provide historical depth. The actions of the ordeal operator invite the viewer to consider how supernatural beliefs, physiological processes and applications of psychology all contribute to the working of the ordeal.

This is one of the most conscientious and respectful collaborations between a filmmaker and an anthropologist who knows the culture intimately.

Bibliography.
Gibbs, James L., Jr. 1965. The Kpelle of Liberia. In *Peoples of Africa,* edited by James L. Gibbs, Jr., pp. 197–240. New York: Holt, Rinehart & Winston.

Dani Houses (1974). 16 min. Made by Karl G. Heider. Distributed by UCEMC.

Follows the construction process of the two sorts of Dani houses, round and rectangular. Shot in 1963, two years after *Dead Birds*, in the same neighborhood of the Grand Valley Dani (West New Guinea, now Irian Jaya, Indonesia). An elemental technology film, made by the anthropologist who had spent two years studying Dani technology.

Bibliography. See bibliography for *Dead Birds*, below, but especially K. G. Heider 1970:252–272.

Dani Sweet Potatoes (1974). 19 min. Made by Karl G. Heider. Distributed by UCEMC.

Follows the sweet-potato cycle of Dani horticulture from clearing the gardens through planting to steaming and eating. Shot in 1963, two years after *Dead Birds*, in the same neighborhood of Grand Valley Dani (West New Guinea, now Irian Jaya, Indonesia). Mainly technology, with some child-rearing sequences.

Bibliography. See bibliography for *Dead Birds*, below, but especially K. G. Heider 1970:31–44.

Dead Birds (1963). 83 min. Made by Robert Gardner. Distributed by Phoenix. Rental by UCEMC, Cont/McG-H, and others.

A film on some Grand Valley Dani of Netherlands New Guinea (now the Indonesian province of Irian Jaya), especially Weyak, a man, and Pua, a boy. The structure of the film follows the events of war and ritual which occurred during the shooting of the film and utilizes the Dani symbolism of man-as-bird as a metaphor for death. Filmed between April and September 1961 in an unpacified part of the Grand Valley of the Balim River.

Bibliography.
Gardner, Robert, and Karl G. Heider. 1969. *Gardens of war: Life and death in the New Guinea stone age*. New York: Random House.
Heider, Karl G. 1970. *The Dugum Dani: A Papuan culture in the highlands of West New Guinea*. Chicago: Aldine.
————. 1972. *The Dani of West Irian: An ethnographic companion to the film "Dead Birds."* New York: Mss Information Corp.
Matthiessen, Peter. 1962. *Under the mountain wall: A chronicle of two seasons in the stone age*. New York: Viking Press.

Desert People (1969). 51 min. Made by Ian Dunlop in collaboration with the anthropologist Robert Tonkinson. Distributed by Cont/McG-H. Rental by UCEMC.

This is part four of the People of the Australian Western Desert Series (see below), and the most general film of the series.

Bibliography.
Tonkinson, Robert. 1974. *The jigalong mob: Aboriginal victors of the desert crusade*. Menlo Park, Calif.: Cummings.

The Feast (1970). 29 min. Made by Timothy Asch, in collaboration with the anthropologist Napoleon Chagnon. Distributed by USNAC. Rental by UCEMC.

An account of the alliance-making gift exchange and feasting between two previously warring villages of Yanomamö Indians, who live in southern Venezuela. The first part of the film is a heavily narrated explanation of what will happen; the main body of the film shows the events of one feast with synchronized sound and an occasional English subtitle. The film was designed to illustrate chapter four of Chagnon's ethnography.

Bibliography.
Chagnon, Napoleon. 1968. *Yanomamö: The fierce people*. New York: Holt, Rinehart & Winston.

Floating in the Air, Followed by the Wind: Thaipusam (1973). Ca. 33 min. Made by Gunther Pfaff in collaboration with the psychiatrist Ronald Simons. Distributed by UCEMC.

An account of the Hindu penitential ceremony performed by Tamils living in Kuala Lumpur, Malaysia. To thank the god or to appeal to the god, individuals go into trance, have pins thrust through their skin, or carry burdens anchored by sharpened hooks inserted into their skin, and walk to a temple. The film uses footage of interviews with penitents and footage of the actual ceremony.

Forty Seven Cents (1973). 25 min. Distributed by UCEMC.

Describes the situation of the Pit River Indians of California, who have been subjected to systematic treaty violations and questionable legal maneuvering, resulting in governmental payments of forty-seven cents per acre as land settlement. Interviews with ineffectual men of goodwill (Ramsey Clark and John Tunney) and with Pit River people themselves.

Grass (1925). 66 min. Made by Merian C. Cooper and Ernest B. Schoedsack. Distributed by UCEMC (rental).

The first part of *Grass* is a banal and dated travelogue. In the second part, the filmmakers follow the Bakhtiari Tribe (of Persia) and their herds on their annual trek from their lowland winter grazing grounds to their summer lands, in search of grass. Certainly one of the most dramatic human experiences ever filmed.

Bibliography.
Cooper, Merian C. 1925. *Grass*. New York: G. P. Putnam's Sons.

Gum Preparation, Stone Flaking; Djagamara Leaves Badjar (1969). 19 min. Made by Ian Dunlop in collaboration with the anthropologist Robert Tonkinson. Distributed by UCEMC.

This film is part two of the series People of the Australian Western Desert (see below).

Gurkha Country: Some Aspects of Fieldwork in Social Anthropology (1967). 19 min. Made by the anthropologists John and Patricia Hitchcock. Distributed by IFB, PSU, and UCEMC.

One of the rare films about fieldwork. Made by the Hitchcocks about their own research and living experiences with the Magars of the Nepal Himalayas.

Bibliography.
Hitchcock, John T. 1966. *The Magars of Banyan Hill*. New York: Holt, Rinehart & Winston.

Hadza: The Food Quest of a Hunting and Gathering Tribe of Tanzania (1966). 40 min. Made by Sean Hudson in collaboration with James Woodburn. Rental by UCEMC.

A view of the Hadza as a hunting and gathering tribe which spent a minimum amount of time in food gathering and had much leisure time to sit around talking and gambling.

Bibliography.
Woodburn, James C. 1968. An introduction to Hadza ecology; Stability and flexibility in Hadza residential groupings. In *Man the hunter*, edited by Richard B. Lee and Irven De Vore, pp. 49–55, 103–110. Chicago: Aldine.

Holy Ghost People (1967). 53 min. Made by Peter Adair. Distributed by Cont/McG-H. Rental by UCEMC.

A view of the white Pentecostal church in Scrabble Creek, West Virginia, whose members enter ecstatic trance, speak in tongues, and handle poisonous snakes to show that they are possessed by the spirit. Introduced by interview sequences in which the people describe their behavior and beliefs, then a long synchronized sound sequence of the prayer meeting itself.

Bibliography.
La Barre, Weston. 1962. *They shall take up serpents: Psychology of the southern snake-handling cult*. Minneapolis: University of Minnesota Press. Paperback ed. New York: Schocken Books, 1969.
Mead, Margaret. 1968. Review of *Holy Ghost people*. *American Anthropologist* 70:655.

The Hunters (1956). 73 min. Made by John Marshall. Distributed by Cont/McG-H. Rental by UCEMC, NYU, PSU, and others.

A story about four Kalahari Desert Bushmen and their search for food for their families. After wounding a giraffe with a poison arrow they track it for days, finally kill it, and bring the meat back to distribute to their people. Essentially a film about the hunting techniques and the hunting knowledge of the Bushmen.

Bibliography.
Lee, Richard B. 1969. !Kung Bushman subsistence: An input-output analy-

sis. In *Environment and cultural behavior*, edited by A. P. Vayda, pp.
47–79. Garden City, New York: Natural History Press.
Marshall, Lorna. 1965. The !Kung Bushmen of the Kalahari Desert. In
Peoples of Africa, edited by James L. Gibbs, pp. 241–278. New York:
Holt, Rinehart & Winston.
Thomas, Elizabeth Marshall. 1959. *The harmless people*. New York: Knopf.
Thompson, William Irwin. 1971. *At the edge of history*. [See chapter 4.]
New York: Harper & Row.

Invisible Walls (1969). 12 min. Made by Richard Cowan and Lucy Turner.
Distributed by UCEMC and PSU.

A filmic demonstration of the principles of personal space and boundaries,
developed by Edward T. Hall under the general label of proxemics. The film
shows an experiment carried out in some Los Angeles shopping centers.
A hidden camera captures people's reactions to the actors when they move
too close, invading the personal space.

Bibliography.
Birdwhistell, Ray L. 1970. Review of *Invisible walls*. *American Anthropologist* 72:724.
Hall, Edward T. 1959. *The silent language*. New York: Doubleday.

An Ixil Calendrical Divination (1966). 32 min. Made by Carroll Williams and
Joan Williams in collaboration with the anthropologists B. N. Colby and L.
Colby. Distributed by Zia.

Among the Ixil Maya of Guatemala, professional diviners will get answers
to their clients' questions by laying out beans in a sort of calendar order as
they are chanting prayers; this process is repeated again and again. The
film uses synchronous sound and, after the introductory shots, shows only
the diviner's hands arranging and rearranging the beans, in order to give
the ceremony in real elapsed time.

Karba's First Years (1952). 19 min. Made by Gregory Bateson and Margaret
Mead in 1936–1938. Distributed by NYU. Rental by UCEMC and others.

Follows the major developmental stages in the infancy of a Balinese boy.

Bibliography. See the bibliography for *Trance and Dance in Bali*, below.

Kypseli: Men and Women Apart (1974). Ca. 40 min. Made by Paul Aratow
and Richard Cowan in collaboration with the anthropologist Susannah Hoffman. Distributed by UCEMC.

A film which closely follows Hoffman's ethnographic study of a Greek island community, emphasizing the many ways in which male and female roles are defined.

The Lion Hunters (1970). 68 min. Made by the anthropologist Jean Rouch. Distributed by Cont/McG-H. Rental by UCEMC.

Made on the upper Niger in West Africa, where farmers and pastoralists intermingle. Some villagers who are professional lion hunters are called in to kill lions which have been raiding the pastoralists' herd. But lion hunting is no casual matter, and the rituals of the hunt are shown in great detail.

Louisiana Story (1948). 77 min. Made by Robert Flaherty, with Richard Leacock as cameraman. Distributed by MOMA. Rental by UCEMC.

A lyrical picture of Cajun life in the Louisiana bayou country.

Bibliography. See Calder-Marshall 1963:211–228.

Ma'Bugi' (1974). 30 min. Shot by the anthropologist Eric Crystal and edited by Lee Rhoades. Distributed by UCEMC.

Follows the major trance ritual (*ma'bugi'*) of a Toraja village in central Sulawesi (Celebes), Indonesia.

Les Maîtres Fous (1953). 30 min. Made by the anthropologist Jean Rouch. Distributed by Cont/McG-H. Rental by UCEMC.

Tribesmen from the upper Niger who have come to Accra for work perform an annual Haouka ceremony, a violent trance performance in which they imitate (and mock) the British colonial government. The film first shows the men of the Haouka at their ordinary jobs, then follows the ceremony, and finally shows them again at their jobs the next day, explicitly suggesting that the cathartic blow-out of the ceremony allows them to tolerate their daily drudgery.

Margaret Mead's New Guinea Journal (1968). 90 min. Made by Craig Gilbert. Distributed by IU. Rental by PSU and UCEMC.

Shows Margaret Mead's 1968 return to Manus, where she had done ethnographic research in the 1920s, the 1950s, and the early 1960s. A rare view of an anthropologist in the field. The film also uses old photographs and footage to give an excellent history of Manus from the German colonial period through the Second World War, and from the postwar nativistic Paliau movement to the preparations for nationhood.

Bibliography.
Mead, Margaret. 1930. *Growing up in New Guinea: A comparative study of primitive education*. New York: William Morrow & Co.
————. 1956. *New lives for old: Cultural transformation—Manus 1928–1953*. New York: William Morrow & Co.
Schwartz, Theodore. 1962. *The Paliau movement in the Admiralties 1946–1954*. American Museum of Natural History Papers, vol. 49, pt. 2.

Maring in Motion: A Choreometric Analysis of Movement among a New Guinea People (1970?). 18 min. Made by Marek Jablonko in collaboration with the anthropologist Alison Jablonko. Distributed by NYU.

A visual version of Alison Jablonko's ethnographic study (unpublished) of movement style—the first systematic application of Alan Lomax's choreometrics to a specific culture.

Matjemosh: A Woodcarver from the Village of Amanamkai—Asmat Tribe on the Southwest Coast of New Guinea (1970?). 27 min. Made by the anthropologist Adrian A. Gerbrands. Rental by UCEMC.

Set on the Asmat Coast of southern West New Guinea (now the Indonesian province of Irian Jaya). Focuses on the personality of Matjemosh, showing him in his cultural and social context, and follows his carving of a drum, going into the symbolic aspects of Asmat art.

Bibliography.
Gerbrands, Adrian A. 1967. *Wow-Ipits: Eight Asmat woodcarvers of New Guinea*. The Hague: Mouton.
Kiefer, Thomas M. 1966. Review of *Matjemosh*. *American Anthropologist* 68.1:300.

Microcultural Incidents in Ten Zoos (1971). 34 min. Made by J. D. Van Vlack in collaboration with the anthropologist Ray L. Birdwhistell. Distributed by PSU.

A filmed version of a Birdwhistell lecture, illustrating the principles of kinesics, using footage from zoos in seven countries to show how people interact, communicate, and express themselves by nonverbal means when confronted with generally similar stimuli (mainly elephants).

Bibliography.
Birdwhistell, Ray L. 1970. *Kinesics and context: Essays on body motion communication*. Philadelphia: University of Pennsylvania Press.

Moana: A Romance of the Golden Age (1926). 85 min. Made by Robert Flaherty. Distributed by MOMA.

Life and culture on Savai'i, Western Samoa. The highlight is the tattooing ceremony for the young man Moana.

Bibliography. Calder-Marshall 1963:98–120.

Mokil (1950). 58 min. Made by Conrad Bentzen. Distributed by SPF. Rental by UCEMC.

A holistic picture of the Micronesian atoll of Mokil, showing the sorts of cultural and social changes which occur as a result of growing population and the shift from subsistence, cooperative economy to cash economy.

Bibliography.

Kiste, Robert C., and Paul D. Schaefer. 1974. Review of *Mokil*. *American Anthropologist* 76.3:715–717.

The Moontrap (1963). 84 min. Made by Pierre Perrault, Michael Brault, and Marcel Carrière. Distributed by Cont/McG-H. Rental by UCEMC.

Set in a French-Canadian community on an island in the St. Lawrence River. Follows the efforts of the villagers to revive the catching of Beluga whales.

Mosori Monika (1970?). 20 min. Made by Chick Strand. Distributed by Cont/McG-H. Rental by UCEMC.

Shows the dilemma of the Warao Indians of Venezuela, caught between their own traditions and pressures to "modernize" and convert to Christianity. The narration speaks in the words of a Warao woman and a Spanish nun.

Nanook of the North (1922). 55 min. Made by Robert Flaherty. Distributed by MOMA and Cont/McG-H. Rental by NYU, PSU, UCEMC, and others.

Vignettes from the life of Nanook, the Eskimo hunter.

Bibliography. Calder-Marshall 1963:76–97.

Navajos Film Themselves Series (1966). Seven films made by Navajos as part of an experiment in semiotics of film, performed by Sol Worth and John Adair. Distributed by NYU.

Bibliography.

Collier, John. 1974. Review of the series. *American Anthropologist* 76.2:481–486.

Worth, Sol, and John Adair. 1972. *Through Navajo eyes: An exploration in film communication and anthropology*. Bloomington: Indiana University Press.

Nawi (1971?). 22 min. Made by David and Judith MacDougall. Distributed by CHF, PSU, UCEMC, and others.

Shows the Jie cattle herders of Uganda as they prepare to go to their dry season camps.

Bibliography.
Gulliver, P. H. 1965. The Jie of Uganda. In *Peoples of Africa*, edited by James L. Gibbs, Jr., pp. 157–196. New York: Holt, Rinehart & Winston.

Netsilik Eskimo Series (late 1960s). Some dozen films, produced by the Educational Development Corporation in collaboration with the anthropologists Asen Balikci and Guy Mary-Rousselière. Distributed by UEVA.

Reconstructed technology of the Pelly Bay (Canada) Netsilik Eskimo. The films were prepared for secondary school educational packages.

Bibliography.
Balikci, Asen, and Quentin Brown. 1966. Ethnographic filming and the Netsilik Eskimos. In *Educational Services Incorporated quarterly report, spring-summer 1966*, pp. 19–33. Newton, Mass.: Educational Services Incorporated.

No Longer Strangers (1966?). Ca. 25 min. Produced and distributed by RBMU.

A missionary account of the conversion of the Western Dani of Irian Jaya, Indonesia. (The Western Dani live just to the west of the Grand Valley Dani of *Dead Birds*.)

Bibliography.
O'Brien, Denise, and Anton Ploeg. 1964. Acculturation movements among the Western Dani. *American Anthropologist* 66.4.2:281–292.

The Nuer (1970). 75 min. Made by Hilary Harris and George Breidenbach with the assistance of Robert Gardner. Distributed by Phoenix, Cont/ McG-H, and UCEMC.

A poetic film concentrating on evocative images of life among a group of Nuer living in Ethiopia. Creates a strong and memorable impression of the people, their cattle, their artifacts, and their land. On occasion, an English narration is used to give a more ethnographic account of events, especially:

a bride-price dispute; a ghost marriage; a revitalistic ceremony intended to combat a smallpox epidemic; and the climax of the film, a *gar* initiation, where two boys receive the forehead incisions of manhood.

Bibliography.

Evans-Pritchard, E. E. 1940. *The Nuer: A description of the modes of livelihood and political institutions of a Nilotic people*. Oxford: Oxford University Press.

Beidelman, T. O. 1966. The ox and Nuer sacrifice. *Man* 1:453–467.

———. 1968. Some Nuer notions of nakedness, nudity and sexuality. *Africa* 38:113–131.

N/um Tchai: The Ceremonial Dance of the !Kung Bushmen (1966). 25 min. Made by John Marshall. Distributed by DER. Rental by UCEMC.

The curing ritual of the Kalahari Bushmen, in which the curers go into trance.

Bibliography.

Lee, Richard B. 1968. The sociology of !Kung Bushman trance perform-ances. In *Trance and possession states*, edited by Raymond H. Prince, pp. 35–54. Montreal: R. M. Bucks Memorial Society.

Marshall, Lorna. 1969. The medicine dance of the !Kung Bushmen. *Africa* 39.4:381–437.

The Path (1972). 34 min. Made by Donald Rundstrom, Ronald Rundstrom, and Clinton Bergum. Distributed by Sumai. Rental by UCEMC.

A film which depicts the Japanese tea ceremony, using the aesthetics of the *way*, or the *do*, to shape the structure of the film. It is "about" balance and energy.

Bibliography.

Rundstrom, Donald; Ronald Rundstrom; and Clinton Bergum. 1973. *Japa-nese tea: The ritual, the aesthetics, the way. An ethnographic companion to the film "The path."* New York: Mss Information Corp.

People of the Australian Western Desert Series (1969). A ten-part series of films made by Ian Dunlop for the Australian Institute of Aboriginal Studies, in collaboration with the anthropologist Robert Tonkinson. Distributed by UCEMC. Rental by PSU.

A series of films concentrating on the subsistence technology of the aborigines of the Western Desert of Australia. The films were shot of a family which had been living at a mission station but agreed to return to the desert with the film crew.

Bibliography.
Tonkinson, Robert. 1974. *The jigalong mob: Aboriginal victors of the desert crusade*. Menlo Park, Calif.: Cummings.

Pomo Shaman (1964). 20 min. [An abridged version of *Sucking Doctor*, which is 45 min. long.] Part of the American Indian film series. Produced and distributed by UCEMC.

Showing the highlights of a curing ceremony performed by Essie Parrish, the last shaman of the Kashia (southwestern) Pomo Indians of California.

Ramparts of Clay (1969). Ca. 60 min. Distributed by C5.

A fictionalized account of life in the Tunisian village which had been described in Duvignaud's ethnography. The film itself was shot in Algeria.

Bibliography.
Duvignaud, Jean. 1970. *Change at Shebika: Report from a North African village*. Translated from the French by Frances Frenaye. New York: Pantheon Books.

Rivers of Sand (1974). 85 min. Made by Robert Gardner. Distributed by Phoenix.

About the Hamar cattle herders of southwestern Ethiopia, emphasizing the life of women and their role in the Hamar society by returning again and again throughout the film to one Hamar woman who describes her life.

Song of Ceylon (1934). 45 min. Made by Basil Wright and John Grierson for the Ceylon Tea Propaganda Board. Distributed by MOMA, and Cont/ McG-H. Rental By UCEMC.

A series of images showing various views of Ceylon and the Buddhist aspects of the culture.

Tidikawa and Friends (1973). Ca. 80 min. Made by Jeff and Su Doring. Distributed by Vision Quest. Rental by UCEMC.

The film evokes a mood of events in the life of the Bedamini of Papua New Guinea.

Bibliography.
Schieffelin, Edward L., and Bambi B. Schieffelin. 1974. Review of *Tidikawa and friends*. *American Anthropologist* 76.3:710–714.

To Find Our Life: The Peyote Hunt of the Huichols of Mexico (1968). 65

min. Made by the anthropologist Peter T. Furst. Distributed by PSU. Rental by UCEMC.

Follows a group of Huichols on their ritual quest for the sacred peyote.

Bibliography.

Furst, Peter T. 1972. To find our life: Peyote among the Huichol Indians of Mexico. In *Flesh of the gods: The ritual use of hallucinogens*, edited by Peter T. Furst, pp. 136–184. New York: Praeger.

La Barre, Weston. 1970. Review of *To find our life*. *American Anthropologist* 72:1201.

Myerhoff, Barbara G. 1974. *Peyote hunt: The sacred journey of the Huichol Indians*. Ithaca, N.Y.: Cornell University Press.

Trance and Dance in Bali (1952). 20 min. Made by Gregory Bateson and Margaret Mead. Distributed by NYU. Rental by UCEMC.

A ritual performance filmed in Bali about 1938. The two protagonists, the witch and the dragon, struggle over good and evil, life and death. Many people go into deep trance, and men turn their swords against themselves.

Bibliography.

Bateson, Gregory, and Margaret Mead. 1942. *Balinese character: A photographic analysis*. Special Publications of the New York Academy of Sciences, vol. 2. New York: New York Academy of Sciences.

Belo, Jane. 1960. *Trance in Bali*. New York: Columbia University Press.

————,ed. 1970. *Traditional Balinese culture*. New York: Columbia University Press.

The Turtle People (1973). 26 min. Shot by the anthropologist Brian Weiss and edited by James Ward. Distributed by B&C Films. Rental by UCEMC.

Made as a visual report of Weiss's ecological ethnographic study of the Miskito Indians of Nicaragua. Explains how the Miskito, who have ridden one economic boom after another and always emerged poorer than before, are now depleting their sea turtle population, their best source of protein, to sell to a canning company.

Bibliography.

Gross, Daniel R. 1974. Review of *The turtle people*. *American Anthropologist* 76:486–487.

The Village (1969). 70 min. Made by Mark McCarty in collaboration with the anthropologist Paul Hockings. Distributed by UCEMC.

Impressions and scenes of the village of Dunquin, County Kerry, Ireland, emphasizing the problems of modernization.

We Believe in Niño Fidencio (1973). Ca. 40 min. Made by the anthropologists Jon Olson and Natalie Olson. Distributed by UCEMC.

An account of a pilgrimage center in northern Mexico—a Catholic cult of the Niño Fidencio, who performed healing acts. Told from the viewpoint of the believers.

Wedding of Palo (1937). 72 min. Made in collaboration with the anthropologist Knud Rasmussen. Distributed by MOMA.

Written by the Danish-Eskimo anthropologist Knud Rasmussen and acted by Eskimos on location in eastern Greenland. Apparently a traditional Eskimo love story. Uses fiction to explore the important aspects of Eskimo emotions and culture.

Yanomamö: A Multi-disciplinary Study (1971?). 45 min. Made by Timothy Asch with the collaboration of the anthropologist Napoleon Chagnon and the geneticist James V. Neel. Distributed by DER. Rental by UCEMC.

The account of a medical research expedition to study the Yanomamö Indians of southern Venezuela, with much general ethnographic background.

Bibliography. See bibliography for *The Feast*, above.

Bibliography

American Anthropological Association
1973   *Professional ethics: Statements and procedures of the American Anthropological Association*. Washington, D.C.: American Anthropological Association.

Asch, Timothy
1972   Ethnographic filming and the Yanomamö Indians. *Sightlines* 5.3:6–17.
1974   Audiovisual materials in the teaching of anthropology from elementary school through college. In *Education and cultural process: Toward an anthropology of education*, edited by George D. Spindler, pp. 463–490. New York: Holt, Rinehart & Winston.

Balikci, Asen, and Quentin Brown
1966   Ethnographic filming and the Netsilik Eskimos. In *Educational Services Incorporated quarterly report, spring-summer 1966*, pp. 19–33. Newton, Mass.: Educational Services Incorporated.

Barrett, S. A.
1961   American Indian films. *Kroeber Anthropological Society Papers* 25:155–162.

Barth, Fredrik
1961   *Nomads of South Persia: The Basseri Tribe of the Khamseh Confederacy*. Boston: Little, Brown & Co.

Bateson, Gregory
1939   *Naven: A survey of the problems suggested by a composite picture of the culture of a New Guinea tribe drawn from three points of view*. 2nd ed. Stanford: Stanford University Press, 1958.
1972   *Steps to an ecology of mind*. 1960. Reprint. New York: Ballantine Books.

Bateson, Gregory, and Margaret Mead
1942   *Balinese character: A photographic analysis*. Special Publications of the New York Academy of Sciences, vol. 2. New York: New York Academy of Sciences.

Behlmer, Rudy
1966   Merian C. Cooper. *Films in Review* 17.1:17–35.

Benedict, Ruth
1934   *Patterns of culture*. New York: Houghton Mifflin.

Birdwhistell, Ray L.
1963   The use of audio-visual teaching aids. In *Resources for the teaching of anthropology*, American Anthropological Association Memoir 95, edited by David G. Mandelbaum, Gabriel W. Lasker, and Ethel M. Albert.
1970   *Kinesics and context: Essays on body motion communication*. Philadelphia: University of Pennsylvania Press.

Broekhuijse, J. Th.
1967   *De Wiligiman-Dani: Een cultureel-anthropologische studie over religie en oorlogvoering in de Baliem-vallei*. Tilburg: H. Gianotten N.V.

Calder-Marshall, Arthur
1963   *The innocent eye: The life of Robert Flaherty*. London: W. H. Allen.

Cancian, Frank
1965   *Economics and prestige in a Maya community*. Stanford: Stanford University Press.

Carpenter, Edmund
1972   Oh, what a blow that phantom gave me! New York: Holt, Rinehart &
        Winston.
Chagnon, Napoleon
1968   Yanomamö: The fierce people. New York: Holt, Rinehart & Winston.
Chapple, Eliot Dismore, and Carleton Stevens Coon
1942   Principles of anthropology. New York: Henry Holt & Co.
Condon, W. S., and W. D. Ogston
1966   Sound film analysis of normal and pathological behavior patterns. Journal
        of Nervous and Mental Disorders 143:338–347.
Cooper, Merian C.
1925   Grass. New York: G. P. Putnam's Sons.
Duvignaud, Jean
1970   Change at Shebika: Report from a North African village. Translated from
        the French by Frances Frenaye. New York: Pantheon Books.
Ekman, P., and W. V. Friesen
1969a   Nonverbal leakage and clues to deception. Psychiatry 32.1:88–106.
1969b   The repertoire of nonverbal behavior: Categories, origins, usage, and
        coding. Semiotica 1.1:49–98.
Evans-Pritchard, E. E.
1940   The Nuer: A description of the modes of livelihood and political institutions
        of a Nilotic people. Oxford: Oxford University Press.
Feld, Steve
1974   Avant propos: Jean Rouch. Studies in the Anthropology of Visual Com-
        munication 1.1:35–36.
Fischer, David Hackett
1970   Historians' fallacies: Toward a logic of historical thought. New York:
        Harper and Row.
Gardner, Robert, and Karl G. Heider
1969   Gardens of war: Life and death in the New Guinea stone age. New York:
        Random House.
Gerbrands, Adrian A.
1967   Wow-Ipits: Eight Asmat woodcarvers of New Guinea. The Hague: Mouton.
Griffith, Richard
1953   The world of Robert Flaherty. New York: Duell, Sloan & Pearce.
Halberstadt, Ira
1974   An interview with Fred Wiseman. Filmmakers Newsletter 7.4:19–25.
Heider, John
1974   Catharsis in human potential encounter. Journal of Humanist Psychology
        14.4:27–47.
Heider, Karl G.
1969   Attributes and categories in the study of material culture: New Guinea
        Dani attire. Man 4.3:379–391.
1970   The Dugum Dani: A Papuan culture in the highlands of West New Guinea.
        Chicago: Aldine.
1972a   The Grand Valley Dani pig feast: A ritual of passage and intensification.
        Oceania 42.3:169–197.

1972b The Dani of West Irian: An ethnographic companion to the film "Dead Birds." New York: Mss Information Corp.
1972c. Ed. Films for anthropological teaching. 5th ed. Washington, D.C.: American Anthropological Association.
1974a The attributes of ethnographic film. Newsletter of the Society for the Anthropology of Visual Communication 5.2:4–6.
1974b Ethnographic films: Lifelong learning 44.21, no. 2, pp. 1–5. Berkeley, Calif.: University of California Extension Media Center.
Kendon, Adam, and Andrew Ferber
1973 A description of some human greetings. In Comparative ecology and behavior of primates, edited by R. P. Michael and J. H. Crook, pp. 1–21. London: Academic Press.
Lee, Richard B., and Irven De Vore
1968 Man the hunter. Chicago: Aldine.
Lévi-Strauss, Claude
1955 Tristes tropiques. [1974 English translation by John and Doreen Weightman.] New York: Atheneum.
Lipton, Lenny
1972 Independent filmmaking. San Francisco: Straight Arrow Books.
Lomax, Alan
1973 Cinema, science, and cultural renewal. Current Anthropology 14.4:474–480.
Loud, Pat, with Nora Johnson
1974 Pat Loud: A woman's story. New York: Coward, McCann & Geoghegan.
Malinowski, Bronislaw
1922 Argonauts of the Western Pacific. New York: E. P. Dutton.
1923 The problem of meaning in primitive languages. In The meaning of meaning, edited by C. K. Ogden and I. A. Richards, pp. 296–336. New York: Harcourt, Brace & World.
1929 The sexual life of savages in north-western Melanesia. New York: Harcourt, Brace & World.
Marshall, John
1958 Man as a hunter. Natural History 67.6:291–309; 7:376–395.
Marshall, Lorna
1957 The kin terminology system of the !Kung Bushmen. Africa 27.1:1–25.
Marshall, Lorna, and Megan Biesele
1974 N/um Tchai: The ceremonial dance of the !Kung Bushmen. A study guide. Somerville, Mass.: Documentary Educational Resources.
Matthiessen, Peter
1962 Under the mountain wall: A chronicle of two seasons in the stone age. New York: Viking.
Mauss, Marcel
1925 The gift: Forms and functions of exchange in archaic societies. [1954 English translation by Ian Cunnison.] London: Cohen & West.
Maybury-Lewis, David
1967 Akwe-Shavante society. Oxford: Clarendon Press.

Mead, Margaret
    1928   *Coming of age in Samoa*. New York: William Morrow & Co.
    1930a   Social organization of Manua. *Bishop Museum Bulletin*, no. 76. Honolulu:
            Bishop Museum.
    1930b   *Growing up in New Guinea: A comparative study of primitive education*.
            New York: William Morrow & Co.
    1935   Sex and temperament in three primitive societies. New York: William
            Morrow & Co.
    1970   The art and technology of field work. In *A handbook of method in cultural
            anthropology*, edited by Raoul Naroll and Ronald Cohen, pp. 246–265.
            Garden City, N.Y.: Natural History Press.
    1972   *Blackberry winter: My earlier years*. New York: William Morrow & Co.
Mead, Margaret, and Frances Cook MacGregor
    1951   *Growth and culture: A photographic study of Balinese childhood*. New
            York: G. P. Putnam's Sons.
Metz, Christian
    1974   *Film language: A semiotics of the cinema*. New York: Oxford University
            Press.
Mugge, Robert
    1974   Film grants. *Filmmakers Newsletter* 7.7:52–57; 7.8:78–82.
Mullen, Pat
    1935   *Man of Aran*. New York: E. P. Dutton.
Murdock, George Peter
    1972   Anthropology's mythology. *Proceedings of the Royal Anthropological
            Institute of Great Britain and Ireland for 1971* (London), pp. 17–24.
Oliver, Douglas L.
    1955   *A Solomon Island society*. Cambridge: Harvard University Press.
O'Reilly, Patrick
    1970   Le "documentaire" ethnographique en Océanie. In *Premier catalogue
            sélectif international de films ethnographiques sur la région du Pacifique*,
            pp. 281–305. Paris: UNESCO.
Pincus, Edward
    1969   *Guide to filmmaking*. New York: New American Library.
Radcliffe-Brown, A. R.
    1922   *The Andaman Islanders*. Cambridge: At the University Press.
Raymond, Alan and Susan
    1973   Filming an American family. *Filmmakers Newsletter* 6.5:19–21.
Read, Kenneth E.
    1965   *The high valley*. New York: Charles Scribner's Sons.
Reichlin, Seth
    1974a   *The meat fight: A study guide*. Somerville, Mass.: Documentary
            Educational Resources.
    1974b   *The wasp nest: A study guide*. Somerville, Mass.: Documentary Educa-
            tional Resources.
    1974c   *Bitter melons: A study guide*. Somerville, Mass.: Documentary Educational
            Resources.
    1974d   *Children throw toy assegais: Film notes*. Somerville, Mass.: Documentary
            Educational Resources.

1974e   *Tug of war: Film notes*. Somerville, Mass.: Documentary Educational
        Resources.
1974f   *The lion game: Film notes*. Somerville, Mass.: Documentary Educational
        Resources.
1974g   *Baobab play: Film notes*. Somerville, Mass.: Documentary Educational
        Resources.
Reichlin, Seth, and John Marshall
1974   *An argument about a marriage: The study guide*. Somerville, Mass.:
        Documentary Educational Resources.
Rouch, Jean
1970   Avant propos. In *Premier catalogue sélectif international de films ethno-
        graphiques sur la région du Pacifique*, pp. 13–20. Paris: UNESCO.
1974   The camera and man. *Studies in the Anthropology of Visual Communica-
        tion* 1.1:37–44.
Rundstrom, Donald; Ronald Rundstrom; and Clinton Bergum
1973   *Japanese tea: The ritual, the aesthetics, the way. An ethnographic
        companion to the film "The Path."* New York: Mss Information Corp.
Scheflen, Albert E.
1973   *Communicational structure: Analysis of a psychotherapy transaction*.
        Bloomington: Indiana University Press.
Skinner, Elliott P., ed.
1972   *Peoples and cultures of Africa*. New York: Natural History Press.
Sorenson, E. Richard
1967   A research film program in the study of changing man. *Current Anthropol-
        ogy* 8.5:443–460.
1974   Anthropological film: A scientific and humanistic resource. *Science*
        186.4169:1079–1085.
Thomas, Elizabeth Marshall
1959   *The harmless people*. New York: Knopf.
Wood, Robin
1971   *The Apu trilogy*. New York: Praeger.
Worth, Sol
1969   The development of a semiotic of film. *Semiotica* 1.3:282–321.
Worth, Sol, and John Adair
1972   *Through Navajo eyes: An exploration in film communication and anthro-
        pology*. Bloomington: Indiana University Press.

Index

Absence, ethnographic, 51
  as attribute dimension, 101. *See also* Presence, ethnographer's
Adair, John, 43, 90, 147–148
Adair, Peter, 143
Alteration of material culture, 55
American Anthropological Association
  ethics statement of, 118–120
  institutional support of film by, 44–45;
"American Family, An," 23, 53, 137
American Indian Series (University of California), 40–41, 137
Anasternaria, 73, 137
Appeals to Santiago, 47, 65, 138
Aratow, Paul, 124, 144–145
Argument about a Marriage, An, 93, 138
  awareness of filmmakers in, 61
  complexity of, 37–38, 93
  high energy in, 69
Asch, Timothy, 36, 38–39, 45, 65, 96, 124, 141, 152
Attributes
  and attribute dimension grid, 112–117
  and attribute profiles of films, 114–115
  and blank attribute dimension grid, 117
  as dimensions, 97–111
  in order of ethnographicness, 112–113
Audience, 92–95
  demands made on, 93
  intended, 92–93
Ax Fight, The, 39

Baboons of Gombe, 138
  whole acts in, 83
Balikci, Asen, 41–42, 57, 148
Barrett, Samuel A., 41, 137
Barth, Fredrik, 131
Baskin, Arnold, 138
Bateson, Gregory, 139, 144, 151
  in Bali and New Guinea, 27–30, 82, 93, 124, 131
  on camera consciousness, 51–52
  nonverbal behavior studies by, 78, 80
  on triggering behavior, 57–58
Behlmer, Rudy, 25
Beidelman, T. O., 149
Belo, Jane, 28, 151

Benedict, Ruth, 18
Bentzen, Conrad, 147
Bergum, Clinton, 8, 44, 65, 97, 103, 149
Biesele, Megan, 37
Birdwhistell, Ray L., 78, 80, 87, 128, 130, 144, 146
Bitter Melons, 138
  remarkable example of closure in, 86
Blunden Harbor, 31
Boas, Franz
  in the Arctic, 18
  ignoring Flaherty, 19
Bourne, Geoffrey H.
  reactions of, to being filmed, 121
Brault, Michael [Michel], 59, 147
Breidenbach, George, 35, 59, 148
Brew, J. O., 31
Broekhuijse, Jan Th., 33–34, 66, 132
Brown, Quentin, 41–42, 57, 148
Bruner, Jerome, 92

Calder-Marshall, Arthur
  opinions of, on Flaherty, 20, 22, 24, 147
California, University of
  American Indian Series, 40–41
  1964 film conference at, 44
Camera consciousness, 50–55
Cancian, Frank, 65, 138
Carpenter, E. R.
  monkey films of, 94
Carpenter, Edmund
  New Guinea experiments of, 52
Carrière, Marcel, 147
Chagnon, Napoleon, 38–39, 96, 124, 141, 152
Chalfen, Richard, 43
Chang, 27
Chapple, Eliot Dismore, 92
Childhood Rivalry in Bali and New Guinea, 29, 94, 96, 139
Choreometric research, 78
Chronicle of a Summer, 39–40, 59, 139
  ethnographers' presence in, 61, 101
  structure of, 39–40
Climax. *See* Peak events
Close-up shots
  as opposed to principle of whole bodies, 76–80

Closure, 85–86. *See also* Whole acts
Colby, B. N., 144
Colby, L., 144
Collaboration between filmmaker and
    anthropologist, 125–127
    Asch and Chagnon and, 38–39
    in *Dead Birds*, 33–34
    lack of, 6, 42
    Rasmussen and, 27
Collier, John, 147–148
Condon, William S., 78, 87
Contextualization of filmed events,
    75–76, 80–81
    in attribute dimension grid, 106
    re whole bodies, 80
Coon, Carleton Stevens, 92
Cooper, Merian C., 25, 27, 131, 142. *See
    also Grass*
Cowan, Richard, 124, 128, 144–145
Cows of Dolo Ken Paye, 81, 82, 139–140
    whole acts in, 84, 108
Credibility of films, 94–95
Crystal, Eric, 145
Curtis, Edward, 20
Cutaway shots
    drawbacks of, 91

Dances of the Kwakiutl, 31
Dani Houses, 62, 140
    attribute dimension analysis of,
        97–111
    attribute dimension profile of, 114–115
    description of time in, 68
    ethnographic absence in, 101
    as generalized account, 13–14
    low energy level in, 99
    point of view of, 65
    relation of, to ethnography, 103, 111,
        124, 132
    sound in, 7
    whole acts in, 83, 125
Dani Sweet Potatoes, 62, 68, 124
    attribute dimension analysis of,
        97–111
    attribute dimension profile of, 114–115
    dilemma of soft focus in, 47–48
    distortion in, 100
    ethnographic absence in, 101
    information load in, 94

    low energy level in, 99
    minimal narration in, 73, 87
    relationship to ethnography of, 96, 103,
        111, 132
    sound in, 7
    structure of, 81–83
    whole acts in, 81–83
Dead Birds, 22
    absence of women in, 12, 75
    alternate interpretations of behavior in,
        33
    attribute dimension analysis of,
        97–111
    attribute dimension profile of, 114–115
    circumstances of production of, 33–34
    closure in, 85
    contextualization in, 75–76
    curious criticisms of, 12, 33, 75
    distortions in, 56, 58, 66–68
    embedded structure of, 82
    generalization in, 88, 132
    high energy level in, 53–54, 99
    narration as patch in, 72
    point of view of, 64
    relation of, to ethnography, 33, 34, 96,
        103, 110–111, 124, 126, 132
    sound in, 70, 105
    story line of, 81–82
    use of, in teaching, 133
    whole acts in, 83
Deetz, James
    as ingenious teacher, 133
Desert People
    acknowledgment of filmmaking
        circumstances in, 58
    collaboration in, 126
    distracting close-ups in, 78
    explaining unrepresentative acts in, 89
DeVore, Irven, 32
Distortions and filmmaking, 49–68
    inevitability of, 49. *See also* Camera
        consciousness; Truth
Division of labor. *See* Collaboration
Doring, Jeff and Su, 56, 150
Dunlop, Ian, 42, 141–142, 149
Duvignaud, Jean, 27, 150

Educational Development Center, 41
Educational Services, Inc., 41

Ekman, P., 78
Elephant Boy, 21
Elisofon, Eliot, 34
Energy level
  in An Argument about a Marriage and
    The Feast, 69
  of ordinary conversation, 80
  relative to camera team, 53–54, 99
Ethical considerations, 118–121
Ethnographic companions to films, 97,
  111, 132
Evaluations of films, 116
Evans-Pritchard, E. E., 35, 131, 149

Feast, The, 65
  collaboration in filmmaking, 96, 126
  high energy level in, 69
  innovative structure of, 38
  relation of, to ethnography, 110, 124
Feld, Steve, 39
Ferber, Andrew, 52, 54
Fictional films
  in exotic locales, 26–27
Fiering, Al, 137
Films for Anthropological Teaching, 5,
  44–45, 96, 130–131, 135
Finances of filmmaking, 121–123
Fischer, David Hackett, 16
Flaherty, Frances
  describes making Moana, 21
Flaherty, Robert, 20–24, 73
  igloo set of, 55
  intensive immersion technique of,
    21–22
  and native feedback story, 23
  neglect of, by contemporary
    anthropologists, 18–19
  as storyteller, 81
  subsidizations of, 63–64, 123
  ventures of, into commercial fictional
    films, 26
  and visual suspense, 23–24, 72, 93
  and whole people, 22, 90. See also
    Moana; Nanook
Floating in the Air, Followed by the Wind,
  142
  English sound track of, 48
Focus, 47–48
Fontaine, Joan, 53

Forty Seven Cents, 142
  English sound track of, 48
Freyer, Ellen, 139
Friesen, W. V., 78
Furst, Peter T., 95, 150–151

Gajdusek, Carleton, 129
Galvin, Frank, 36, 86, 138
Gardner, Robert, xi, 30–37, 59, 64,
  66–68, 70, 75–76, 81, 83, 85, 132,
  140–141, 148, 150
  and generalizations in film, 67
  making Dead Birds, xi, 33–34. See
    also Dead Birds
Generalization on film, 6, 87–89
  in The Nuer, 88. See also
    Reconstruction
Gerbrands, Adrian A., 61, 89, 146
Gibbs, James L., Jr., 81, 84, 139–140
Gibson, Gordon, 45
Gilbert, Craig, 137, 145–146
Goodall, Jane, 138
Goulart, Ron, 137
Grants, filmmaking, 123
Grass
  behavior out of context in, 76, 97
  and ethnography, 110–111, 131
  production of, 25
Grierson, John, 63, 82, 150
Griffith, Richard, 20, 21, 23
Gross, Daniel R., 151
Gulliver, P. H., 148
Gum Preparation, Stone Flaking, 142
  careful qualifications in, 89
Gurkha Country, 60, 142–143

Haddon, Alfred C., 20
Hadza
  collaboration in production of, 126–127
  and relationship to ethnography, 72
  wordy narration of, 105
Halberstadt, Ira, 120
Hall, Edward T., 144
Hamburg South Sea Expedition
  (1908–1910), 19–20
Harder They Come, The
  as ethnography, 5
Harris, Hilary, 34–35, 148

Harvard Peabody Expedition, 33–34.
    See also Dead Birds
Harvard University
    film activity around, 30–39
Heick, William, 137
Heider, John
    on catharsis, 85
Heider, Karl G., xi, 13–15, 33–34, 54–55,
    62, 66–68, 70, 86, 96–97, 103,
    112, 130–132, 135, 140–141. See
    also Dani Houses; Dani Sweet
    Potatoes
Heusch, Luc de, 39
Hitchcock, Alfred, 53
Hitchcock, John T. and Patricia, 60,
    142–143
Hockings, Paul, 61, 151–152
Hoffman, Susannah, 65, 124, 144–145
Holism
    and film, 74–81, 125
    as principle of ethnography, 6–7. See
        also Whole acts; Whole bodies;
        Whole people
Holy Ghost People, 143
    close-up shots in, 78, 107
Hudson, Sean, 143
Hunters, The, 22, 31–33, 102, 143–144
    contextual interaction in, 80–81
    criticism of, 31–32
    reconstruction of giraffe hunt in, 12, 67
    relation of, to ethnography, 103
    remarkable closure in, 85–86, 108
    whole acts in, 108

Institute for Aboriginal Studies
    (Australia), 122
Intensive immersion
    Flaherty's technique of, 21–22
Interruption of behavior in filmmaking,
    55–56
In the Land of the War Canoes, 20
Invisible Walls, 128, 144
Ixil Calendrical Divination, An,
    close-up in, 83
    real time in, 68, 102

Jablonko, Alison, 128, 146
Jablonko, Marek, 128, 146
Johnson, Martin and Osa, 20

Johnson, Nora, 53, 137
Joking Relationship, 81
Jones, C. A., 45
Jump cuts, 49

Karba's First Years, 144
    as unique longitudinal film, 82
Kendon, Adam, 80
    on camera consciousness, 52, 54
Kiefer, Thomas M., 146
King Kong
    as ethnography and primatology, 27
Kiste, Robert C., 147
Kroeber, A. L., 128
Kypseli, 144–145
    collaboration in production of, 124, 126
    theoretical analysis in, 65

La Barre, Weston, 143, 151
Land, The, 21
Last Picture Show, The
    as ethnography, 5
Leacock, Richard, 145
Lee, Richard B., 32, 143–144, 149
Levin, G. Roy, 139
Lévi-Strauss, Claude, 61
Lion Hunters, The, 40, 145
    wordy narration in, 105
Lipton, Lenny, 118
Lomax, Alan, 78, 80, 146
Loud, Pat, 23, 53, 137
Louisiana Story, 21, 64, 145

Ma'Bugi', 145
Macauley, Cameron, 137
McCarty, Mark, 61, 151–152
    as ebullient cameraman, 54
MacDougall, David and Judith, 69, 148
MacGregor, Frances Cook, 28
McPhee, Colin, 28
Maîtres Fous, Les, 145
    high energy level in, 53–54, 99
    structure of, 40
    theoretical analysis in, 65, 73
    wordy narration in, 105
Malinowski, Bronislaw, 15, 18, 51
    and ethnographic reconstruction,
        12–13
    and "phatic communion," 69

Man Called "Bee", A, 39–60
Man of Aran, 21
Margaret Mead's New Guinea Journal,
    60, 145–146
Maring in Motion, 128, 146
Marshall, Elizabeth, 31. *See also*
    Thomas, Elizabeth Marshall
Marshall, John, 61, 81, 97, 138,
    143–144, 149
  making *The Hunters*, 30–33
  and new Bushman films, 36–39
  use of closure, 85–86. *See also The
    Hunters*
Marshall, Laurence K., 31
Marshall, Lorna, 31, 36, 81, 144,
    149
Matjemosh, 89, 109, 146
Matthiessen, Peter, 34, 66, 132, 141
Mauss, Marcel, 65
Maybury-Lewis, David, 51
Mead, Margaret, 139, 143–144, 151
  in Bali and New Guinea, 27–30, 82, 93,
    124, 131
  on camera consciousness, 51–52
  in Samoa, 18–19. *See also Margaret
    Mead's New Guinea Journal*
Melies, Gaston, 20
Metz, Christian, 90
Metzger, Duane, 138
Microcultural Incidents in Ten Zoos, x,
    128, 146
Moana, 20–21, 81, 147
  reconstruction in, 26
  visual suspense in, 24
Mokil, 147
  contextualization in, 76, 106
  successful complexity of, 76
Moontrap, The, 147
  explicitness of reconstruction of, 59,
    101
Morin, Edgar, 39, 61, 139
Mosori Monika, 94, 147
Mugge, Robert, 123
Mugging, 54
Mullen, Pat, 23
Murdock, George Peter, 31
Murnau, F. W., 26
Music in sound track, 74, 104
Myerhoff, Barbara G., 151

Nanook, 20–24, 26, 63, 81, 94
  two versions of, compared, 24, 93,
    104–105
  unusual igloo of, 55
  visual suspense in, 24
  and whole people, 90, 109
Narration, 70–74
  attribute dimension of, 105
National Anthropological Film Center
    (Smithsonian Institution), 45, 129
National Film Board (Canada), 122
Navajo film themselves, 43, 147–148
Navajo Silversmith, 43
Nawi, 148
  "phatic communion" in, 69
  sound in, 104
Neel, James V., 152
Netsilik Eskimo films
  collaboration in production of, 126
  design of, 92
  history of, 41–42
  inoffensive costumes in, 94
  natural sound in, 70, 72
  problem of reconstruction in, 57, 60,
    100
  visual suspense in, 73
  whole acts in, 81
No Longer Strangers, 148
  point of view of, compared with *Dead
    Birds*, 64
Nuer, The, 62, 94, 98, 148
  circumstances of production of, 35, 59
  close-up shots in, 78–79, 107
  incomplete acts in, 85
  lack of context in, 76, 106
  lack of ethnographic insight in, 6, 35,
    78–79, 82, 86, 108, 124
  native statements in, 62, 69
  relation of, to printed ethnography,
    111, 131
  structure of, 82–83
  use of, in teaching, 131–132
  visual generalization in, 88. *See also*
    Evans-Pritchard, E. E.
N/um Tchai, 149
  innovative structure of, 37–38

O'Brien, Denise, 148
Ogston, W. D., 78

Oliver, Douglas L., 88
Olson, Jon and Natalie, 152
O'Reilly, Patrick, 19–20

Parrish, Essie, 41, 150
Particularizing, 87–89. *See also*
    Generalization
Path, The, 149
    circumstances of production, 44, 56
    deceptive reality in, 55
    demands on audience by, 93
    energy in, 8, 83
    real time in, 68, 102
    selection in filmmaking, 8, 65, 83, 100
    and written materials, 62, 97, 103, 111
Pather Panchali
    as ethnography, 27
Peak events, 85
    in Bali films, 28
    in scripted films, 27
    in *The Nuer*, 83–84
People of the Australian Western Desert,
    72, 149–150
Perrault, Pierre, 147
Perri, David, 137
Pfaff, Gunther, 142
Pincus, Edward, 118
Ploeg, Anton, 148
Pomo Shaman, 41, 73, 137, 150
Presence, ethnographer's, 60–62. *See
    also* Absence, ethnographic
"Primate"
    controversy around, 121
    lack of understanding in, 108
    lack of whole acts in, 84
Program in Ethnographic Film, 44–45
Propaganda film, 63
Putnam, Samuel, 34

Radcliffe-Brown, A. R., 18
Radio Bantu, 64
Ramparts of Clay, 27, 150
Rango, 27
Rasmussen, Knud, 42
    and Netsilik Eskimo, 42
    and *Wedding of Palo*, 27, 56–57, 152
Ravicz, Robert, 138
Ray, Satyajit, 27

Raymond, Alan and Susan, 53, 137
Read, Kenneth E., 61
Rebecca
    home movies in, 53
Reconstruction in film, 12–14
    in American Indian Series, 40–41
    by Flaherty, 22–23
Reichlin, Seth, 37, 97, 138–139
Research footage, 128
Rhoades, Lee, 145
Rivers of Sand, 150
    circumstances of production of, 35–36
    complex subject matter of, 76, 106
    native statements in, 69
    role of women in, 12
    sound track in, 104–105
Rockefeller, Michael, 34, 70
Rosch, Eleanor, 34
Rose, Ernest, 137
Rouch, Jean, 19, 59, 73, 101, 105, 139,
    145
    attitude of, toward production
        collaboration, 126
    as leader of the French movement,
        39–40. *See also Chronicle of a
        Summer; Les Maîtres Fous*
Roussellet, Guy Marie de, 41
Ruby, Jay, 44–45
Rundstrom, Donald and Ronald, 8, 44,
    55, 65, 83, 97, 103, 149. *See also
    The Path*

Sandall, Roger, 42
Scenes from a Marriage
    as ethnography, 5
Schaefer, Paul D., 147
Scheflen, Albert E., x
Schieffelin, Edward L. and Bambi B., 150
Schoedsack, Ernest B., 142
Schwartz, Theodore, 146
Semiotics, 90–92
    behind the Navajo project, 43
Silverman, Marvin, 81, 84, 139–140
Simons, Ronald, 142
Skinner, Elliott P., 32
Sky Above and the Mud Below, The
    staging in, 57
Smith, Clyde, 137

Smithsonian Institution, 129
Society for the Anthropology of Visual
    Communication, 44–45
Song of Ceylon, 63, 82, 150
Sorenson, E. Richard, 45, 129
Sound, 48–49
    absence of, in *Dani Houses*, 7
    as attribute dimension, 104
    synchronous, 68–70. *See also* Music;
        Narration
Spencer, Baldwin
    as pioneer, 19, 42
"Staged" behavior, 56, 57
Strand, Chick, 94–95, 147
Structure, film, 81–87
Sucking Doctor, 41

Tabu, 26
Teaching, films in, 130–134
Third Man, The, 66
Thomas, Elizabeth Marshall, 31–32, 144
Thompson, William Irwin, 144
Tidikawa and Friends, 150
    relation of, to ethnography, 97,
        110–111, 132
    use of two cameras in, 56
Time represented in film
    real time and film time, 68, 83
Titicut Follies, 36
*To Find Our Life: The Peyote Hunt of the
    Huichols of Mexico*, 95, 150–151
Tokyo Story, 5
Tonkinson, Robert, 141–142, 149–150
Trance and Dance in Bali, 151
    avoidance of close-up in, 107
    freeze frames in, 68
    music in, 74
    shooting speed in, 30
Triggering behavior, 57–60
Truth
    and distortions, 49–50
    in film versus ethnography, 11–15
    and generalizations, 67
    as goal of ethnography, 7
    and points of view, 63–66
    and reconstruction, 13
Turner, Lucy, 128, 144
Turtle People, The, 4, 124, 151

faceless masses in, 109
materialistic approach in, 65, 89
sound track of, 48, 95
unjustified disbelief in, 95

Understanding, ethnographic, 123–125
Unvanquished, The, 27

Van Dyke, W. S., 26
Van Lawick, Hugo, 83, 138
Van Vlack, J. D., 146
Versteegh, Chris, 34
Videotape
    the prospects of, 17, 127–128
Village, The, 151–152
    interview technique in, 61
    intrusion of camera crew in, 54, 99
    music in, 74, 104
Visual suspense
    in Netsilik films, 42
    as used by Flaherty, 23–24

Ward, James, 151
We Believe in Niño Fidencio, 73, 152
Wedding of Palo, 152
    plot of, 27, 56–57
    storytelling sequence in, 81
Weiss, Brian, 89, 151
Wharton, Robert, 137
White Dawn, 27
White Shadows in the South Seas, 26
Whole acts, 82–86
    as attribute dimension, 108
    as dictum, 7, 125
    and structure, 81
Whole bodies, 76–80
    as attribute dimension, 107
    versus close-up shots, 76–79
    as dictum, 7, 125
Whole people, 89–90
    as attribute dimension, 109
    as dictum, 7, 125
    Flaherty's use of, 22. *See also* Holism
Williams, Carroll, 45, 73, 83, 144
Williams, Joan, 144
Wilson, Carter, 138
Winter Sea-Ice Camp, 42
Wiseman, Frederick, 36

attitude of, toward his subjects, 120
   in controversy over "Primate," 84, 121
Woodburn, James, 143
*Wooden Box: Made by Steaming and
   Bending*, 76, 137

World of Apu, The, 27
Worth, Sol, 43, 45, 90, 147–148
Wright, Basil, 63, 82, 150